HOW TO WRITE A DAMN GOOD NOVEL

HOW TO
WRITE A
DAMN GOOD NOVEL

JAMES N. FREY

St. Martin's Press • New York

Design by Jaya Dayal

Library of Congress Cataloging-in-Publication Data
Frey, James N.
  How to write a damn good novel.

  1. Fiction—Technique. I. Title.
PN3365.W37 1987   808.3   87–16343
ISBN 0–312–01044–3

10 9 8 7

To my students at the
University of California, Berkeley, Extension

CONTENTS

▶ What's the who? ▶ Subspecies of *Homo Fictus.*
▶ Creating wonderfully rounded characters, or, how to play
God. ▶ Making characters sizzle. ▶ Building character from
the ground up: the fictional biography. ▶ Interviewing a
character, or, getting to know him the easy way. ▶ At the
character's core: the ruling passion, and how to find it. ▶ The
steadfast protagonist, heartbeat of the dramatic novel.
▶ Stereotyped characters and how to avoid them. ▶ Character
maximum capacity and the "would he really" test.

▶ The how and why of conflict: bringing a character to life.
▶ Equalizing the forces of opposition. ▶ The bonding
principle, or, keeping your characters in the crucible.
▶ Inner conflict and the necessity thereof. ▶ Patterns of
dramatic conflict: static, jumping, and slowly rising.
▶ Genres, the pigeonholes of literature.

▶ Dialogue: direct and indirect, inspired and uninspired.
▶ Dramatic modes.   ▶ The shape of the dramatic scene.
▶ Developing a dramatic scene from the familiar and flat to the
fresh and wonderful.   ▶ How to make a good exchange of
dialogue out of a not-so-good one.   ▶ The commandments of
dynamic prose.   ▶ Prose values beyond the senses.

▶ The why and the what of rewriting.   ▶ Writers' groups and
how to use them.   ▶ Getting along without a good group.
▶ Self-analyzing your story, step by step.

▶ On becoming a novelist.   ▶ What counts most—and it ain't
talent.   ▶ The mathematics of novel writing, or, to get there,
keep plugging even if you've got a hangover.   ▶ What to do
when your muse takes a holiday.   ▶ What to do when the job
is done.

Acknowledgments

THANKS to my wife, Elizabeth, who put up with so much and helped so much with the manuscript; to Lester Gorn, who taught me most of it; to John Berger, who kept asking me the important questions; to my editor at St. Martin's, Brian DeFiore, for being patient and astute; to my agent, Susan Zeckendorf, for her faith; and to the late Kent Gould, who pushed hard to get me started writing *How to Write a Damn Good Novel*. He was a damn good friend.

Introduction

A "DAMN GOOD NOVEL" is intense, and to be intense, a novel must be dramatic. A dramatic novel embodies the following characteristics: it focuses on a central character, the protagonist, who is faced with a dilemma; the dilemma develops into a crisis; the crisis builds through a series of complications to a climax; in the climax the crisis is resolved. Novels such as Ernest Hemingway's *The Old Man and the Sea*, John Le Carre's *The Spy Who Came in from the Cold*, Ken Kesey's *One Flew over the Cuckoo's Nest*, Vladimir Nabokov's *Lolita*, Mario Puzo's *The Godfather*, Charles Dickens's *A Christmas Carol*, and Gustave Flaubert's *Madame Bovary* are all written in the dramatic form and are all damn good novels.

Virginia Woolf's *Mrs. Dalloway* is a classic novel, a finely crafted work of art, well worth reading. It is not, however, in the form of the dramatic novel. Neither is James Joyce's *Ulysses*, a hallmark of twentieth-century English literature. If you wish to write like James Joyce or Virginia Woolf and create experimental, symbolic, philosophical, or psychological novels that eschew the dramatic form, this book is not for you. Nor is it for you if you're looking for an academic critique of the traditional dramatic novel. This is a how-to book on the art of the dramatic novel and does not claim to be anything else.

1.

WHAT IT'S ALL ABOUT
IS "WHO"

WHAT'S THE WHO?

IF YOU can't create characters that are vivid in the reader's imagination, you can't create a damn good novel. Characters are to a novelist what lumber is to a carpenter and what bricks are to a bricklayer. Characters are the *stuff* out of which a novel is constructed.

Fictional characters—*homo fictus*—are not, however, identical to flesh-and-blood human beings—*homo sapiens*. One reason for this is that readers wish to read about the exceptional rather than the mundane. Readers demand that *homo fictus* be more handsome or ugly, ruthless or noble, vengeful or forgiving, brave or cowardly, and so on, than real people are. *Homo fictus* has hotter passions and colder anger; he travels more, fights more, loves more, changes more, has more sex. Lots more sex. *Homo fictus* has more of everything. Even if he is plain, dull, and boring, he'll be more extraordinary in his plainness, dullness, and boringness than his real-life counterparts.

Real human beings are fickle, contrary, wrong-headed—happy one minute, despairing the next, at times changing emotions as often as they take a breath. *Homo fictus, on the other hand, may be complex, may be volatile,* even mysterious, but he's always fathomable. When he isn't, the reader closes the book, and that's that.

Another reason the two species are not identical is that, because of space limitations, *homo fictus* is simpler, just as life is more simple in a story than it is in the real world.

If you were to write down everything that went on with you while you were, say, eating breakfast this morning, you could fill a fat volume—if you included all the millions of sensory impressions, thoughts, and images bouncing around in your head. When depicting the life of a fictional character, a novelist must choose to include only those impressions, thoughts, reflections, sensations, feelings, desires, and so on, that bear on the character's motivations, development, and decision-making faculties—those aspects of character that will affect the way in which the character copes with the dilemmas he will face in the story.

The result of this selection process is the formation of characters who, although they are lifelike, are not whole human beings. *Homo fictus* is an abstraction meant to project the essence, but not the totality, of *homo sapiens*.

SUBSPECIES OF HOMO FICTUS

There are two types of *homo fictus*. The simpler type is called "flat," "cardboard," or "uni-dimensional." These characters are used for the "walk-on" parts. They walk on, say a line or two, and that's that. They are the waiters, newspaper carriers, doormen, bartenders, bellhops. They may be colorful or nondescript; at a high emotional pitch or placid. But they are always peripheral, never central; the reader's interest in them is fleeting. They are easily labeled characters who seem to have only one trait: they are greedy, or pious, or cowardly, or servile, or horny, and so on. They may startle, enlighten, or amuse for a moment, but they have no power to engage the reader's interest for a protracted period of time. They have no depth; the writer does not explore their motives or inner conflicts—their doubts, misgivings, feelings of guilt. As long as uni-dimensional characters are used only for the minor roles in your novel, okay. But when they are used for major roles, such as the principal villain, dramatic writing turns into melodrama.

The other broad type of character is called "rounded," "full-bodied," or "three-dimensional," All the major characters in your novel should be of this type, even the villains. Rounded characters are harder to label. They have complex motives and conflicting desires and are alive with passions and ambitions. They have committed great sins and have borne agonizing sufferings; they are full of worries, woes, and unresolved grievances. The reader has a strong sense that they existed long before the novel began, having lived rich and full lives. Readers desire intimacy with such characters because they are worth knowing.

CREATING WONDERFULLY ROUNDED CHARACTERS, OR, HOW TO PLAY GOD

George Baker, in *Dramatic Technique* (1919), claims that "great drama depends on a firm grasp and sure presentation of complicated character . . . thus the old statement 'Know Thyself' becomes for the dramatist 'know your characters as intimately as possible.' "

Now then, how do you go about getting to know your character "as intimately as possible"?

Lajos Egri, in his essential and remarkable book, *The Art of Dramatic Writing* (1946), describes a rounded character as being three-dimensional. The first dimension he calls the *physiological*; the second, the *sociological*; the third, the *psychological*.

The physiological dimension of a character includes a character's height, weight, age, sex, race, health, and so on. Where would Jim Thorpe have been, for example, had he been born with a club foot? or Marilyn Monroe, had she turned out flat-chested? Or Hank Aaron, had he had a withered arm? Or Barbra Streisand, a small voice? Obviously, not only would their choices of profession have been affected, but their personalities would have been shaped differently as well. A small man cannot "throw his weight around" as a large man can. Pretty or ugly, short or tall, thin or fat—all of these physical traits affect the way a character would have developed, just as such physical traits affect real people.

Society shapes our character based on our appearance, size, sex, build, skin color, scars, deformities, abnormalities, allergies, posture, bearing, lilt in the voice, sweetness of breath, tendency to sweat, nervous ticks and gestures, and so on. A petite, delicate, golden-haired girl with big blue eyes grows up with a completely different set of expectations about what she's going to get out of life than her needle-nosed, bug-eyed sister. To develop a fully rounded character, you must understand the character's physiology completely.

The second of Egri's three dimensions of character is the sociological. What is the character's social class? What kind of a neighborhood did he grow up in? What kind of schools did he attend? What kind of politics did he acquire? Which church nourished his spirit, if any? What were his parents' attitudes about sex, money, getting ahead? Was he given a lot of freedom or none? Was discipline lax or harsh, or somewhere in between? Did the character have lots of friends or few; what kind were they? A Missouri farm boy has grown up in another country from a kid in New York's Spanish Harlem. To understand a character completely you must be able to trace the source of his traits to their roots. Human character is forged by the sociological climate in which an individual is nurtured, whether it's a real human being or a fictional character. Unless the novelist understands the dynamics of the character's development, the character's motivations cannot be fully understood. It is the characters' motivations that produce the conflicts and generate the narrative tension that your novel must have if it is to succeed in holding the reader's attention.

The psychological, Egri's third dimension of character, is the product of the physiological and the sociological dimensions. Within the psychological dimension we find phobias and manias, complexes, fears, inhibitions, patterns of guilt and longing, fantasies, and so on. The psychological dimension includes such things as IQ, aptitudes, special abilities, soundness of reasoning, habits, irritability, sensibility, talents, and the like.

To write a novel you need not be a psychologist. You do not have to have read Freud or Jung or Dear Abby, nor must you be able to discern the difference between a psychopath and a schizophrenic. But you must be a student of human nature and acquire an understanding of *why* people do what they do and say what they say. Try making the world your laboratory. When the secretary in your office quits, ask her why. Your friend wants a divorce; listen to her complaints. Why did your dentist take up a profession that inflicts pain on others and requires him to be nosing around in people's mouths all day? Mine thought he could get rich that way, but so far he can't keep ahead of the payments on his drilling equipment. It's amazing what people will tell you if you ask politely and listen sympathetically. Many novelists keep journals or make character sketches of people they meet, which is a good idea. Grace Metalious, it's been said, peopled *Peyton Place* with friends and neighbors in her hometown, and everybody she knew had no trouble figuring out who all those rakish, bed-hopping characters were. She lost a few friends, got the cold shoulder from a few neighbors, but wrote a damn good novel.

MAKING CHARACTERS SIZZLE

If your novel is not only to succeed, but to be electric, you need to people it with dynamic rather than static characters. A character can be fully-rounded yet be too passive, too mamby-pamby. Characters who can't act in the face of their dilemmas, who run away from conflict, who retreat and suffer without struggling, are not useful to you. They are static, and most of them should meet an untimely death before they ever appear in the pages of your novel and ruin everything. Dramatic novels require dynamic characters, alive with great passions and strong emotions: lust, envy, greed, ambition, love, hate, vengefulness, malice, and the like. Make your characters, at least your major characters, emotional firestorms.

BUILDING CHARACTER
FROM THE GROUND UP:
THE FICTIONAL BIOGRAPHY

In *Fiction Is Folks* (1983), Robert Peck gives the following advice:

> Writing is one heck of a rough racket, which means that if you do it dog lazy, it will defeat you quicker than boo. So, before you type *Chapter One* at the top

of a Virginal Page (and then sit there for a week while
you wonder what to do next) do your homework for
each one of your characters.

"Doing your homework" means creating a background for the
major characters: in effect, writing their biographies. For most
writers, and certainly all beginning writers, character biographies
are a necessary preliminary step in the making of a novel.

Suppose you want to write a murder mystery. You don't
have a plot yet, or even an idea for one. The first thing you
need in a murder mystery is a murderer. The murderer will
be the villain and antagonist of the novel. In a mystery, the
story stems from the machinations of the villain. In a sense,
the villain is the "author" of your story. The cast of characters
you will need in your novel will depend upon your villain's
scheme.

Say you have a notion of a woman who murders her husband
because he has disgraced the family by selling dope to finance
his addiction to betting on slow horses. You have no idea who
this woman is or what she is like, but you know she is a clever
woman (otherwise she is not a worthy antagonist). You know she
will plan the crime with great care and cunning. Her cunning,
moreover, will determine the degree of difficulty the detective
will have, so you'll want her to be as clever as you can make
her.

The second thing you need is someone to solve the crime, the
protagonist. You may at the moment not have anyone in mind
to play the part. What do you do then?

There are many different types of detectives in such novels.
He or she can be a hard-boiled pro (Philip Marlowe, Sam Spade),
a cerebral pro (Sherlock Holmes, Hercule Poirot), a gifted amateur (Ellery Queen, Miss Marple), or a bystander who gets drawn
into the mystery (the second Mrs. de Winter in Daphne du
Maurier's *Rebecca*).

Your decision will depend on the type of novel you envision. Detective fiction offers readers many delights. One might be the delight of watching a great thinker at work. Another might be sharing the bafflement and terror of an innocent caught up in murderous intrigue. Or watching a tough-guy detective slogging through the mud and mire on the seamy side of town, bashing heads and ducking bullets as he goes.

If you're an aficionado of one type, that's what you should be writing. Write the kind of book you like to read. The exception to that rule is the tough-guy detective novel written in the first person. It is a difficult prose style, especially for a beginner. When it's not done well, it comes off as imitative; or worse, as parody.

Whichever type of novel you select, you will be writing in a tradition, and it's best if you've read widely in that tradition and are thoroughly familiar with its conventions. An established writer may depart from convention and his readers will forgive the departure, but a beginner will not enjoy this privilege and is hereby warned to stay within the bounds of accepted practice.

Let's say you decide to write about a pro detective because you enjoy reading Erle Stanley Gardner, Ed McBain, Ross MacDonald, John Dickenson Carr, and Robert B. Parker. The "pro" detective is your favorite kind of detective. But you have no idea what your pro might be like. A good place to start is with a name, which might give you a mental image.

Let's not give him a typical detective's name like Rockford, Harper, Archer, or Marlowe. You want something fresh and different, but nothing far out. Nothing like Stempski Scyzakzk, which you fear might turn your reader off. The idea is to be creative within accepted form, as an architect will change the corners, pillars, slope of the roof, yet still have all the bedrooms, bathrooms and closets his clients have come to expect.

Let's call your detective something that sounds un-detectiveish, like, say, Boyer. Boyer Mitchell, how's that? Good as any. If you can't think of a name, the phone book is full of them. A lot of detectives are middle-aged, tough, grizzled, and experienced. For novelty's sake, let's make Boyer young and inexperienced. Physically, he should not be a typical detective either. Fictional detectives are often tall, handsome in a rugged way, and brash. Let's make Boyer small-boned and gangly, medium height, intelligent-looking, and let's give him large, dark, penetrating eyes and make him round-shouldered and rather slow in his movements. He believes, let's say, in dressing well to make the best impression possible, is well groomed, and has large, sparkling teeth. He has a pleasant manner—quiet and thoughtful. Most people would take him to be a scholar. He's twenty-six and single.

Where did this picture of Boyer Mitchell come from? He was made up out of thin air by the author of the book you are reading, as the book was being drafted, selecting features that are the antithesis of those of most detective characters—features that have become stereotypes. Boyer could just as easily be old, fat, and alcoholic. Your decisions on what characteristics to include in your characters should be based primarily on two considerations: breaking stereotypes and good orchestration.

Good orchestration, according to Lajos Egri, is the art of creating characters with contrasting traits so they are "instruments which work together to give a well-orchestrated composition." In other words, don't make all your characters, say, greedy or ambitious. Characters should serve as foils for one another. If one is excessively studious, another might be excessively lazy in his studies. Hamlet was indecisive; he lacked will, being prone to thinking rather than acting. He brooded, sulked, and felt sorry for himself. His foil, Laertes, was a tough man of action.

One other consideration, when it comes to making up characters, is that you, the writer, will have to live inside the heads of your characters for a long time. You should ask yourself whether you really want to work with these characters. Are they characters you find interesting? Maybe you wouldn't want to work with Boyer Mitchell if he was old, fat, and alcoholic, for no other reason than that you prefer him to be young, small-boned, intelligent, and so on. That's okay, it's your book. If you are fascinated by your characters and like them, it is more likely your readers will too.

So far we have determined some of Boyer's *physiological* dimension and have a hint of his *sociological* dimension. We are starting to get a picture of what he is like, but it's still nebulous. We will need to penetrate his character and really get to know him, for he is to be the star of this novel.

We could start by asking, since he doesn't seem like the typical detective, just how did Boyer get into this business? Perhaps he got into it the way many other young men get into business— by following in his father's footsteps. Here's where you can let your imagination run. Let's say his father was the famous "Big Jake" Mitchell, who was the model Dashiell Hammett used to create the character of Sam Spade. Big Jake was tough, ruthless, and shrewd; he would stop at nothing to protect a client's interest. More than once he broke a jaw in the service of what he called "higher justice." Boyer regards his father as having been something of a bully, but he did admire him. He believes in justice just as strongly as his father did, but he also believes that civilization depends on respect for the law.

Choosing such a father for Boyer would compel him to live up to Big Jake's high standards. People would always be comparing him to his father. Old enemies would still be trying to even scores with the father by making life miserable for the son. Big Jake, even though he's gone, would be a cross for Boyer to bear. When creating a character's biography, look for elements that will influence the character's emotions and behavior in the story. Rounded characters will have a past, and, just like real people, the past will still be with them.

We as yet have only a rough sketch of Boyer Mitchell. We need to flesh him out. We can do that by writing a complete biography of him, either in third person or first person. A biography such as the one that follows is not a story. It may, as this one does, meander a little, give snatches of relationships which are not explored, allude to unexplained events, and so on. Such biographies are not intended to be encyclopedic presentations of the character. A character biography is a brief summary of the character's life to give the writer a better understanding of the character. It is for the writer's use only. Here, written in first person, is Boyer's:

I was born Boyer Bennington Mitchell on the first of January. I'm twenty-six. Not only am I young, I'm young-*looking*. That makes it difficult for me to get respect in my profession, but I've learned to live with it.

What counts with me is getting the job done. That's the one thing I learned from my father. You take somebody's money, you owe them your best work.

My father was "Big Jake" Mitchell. That's another of my problems. It's difficult to live up to a legend like that.

My mother's the one who named me "Boyer Bennington." She was born into an upper-class family—a Bennington of the Vermont Benningtons. Very old New England family. It so happened that in 1955 one of her uncles was murdered here in San Francisco and the police couldn't solve the crime. Big Jake to the rescue. He nabbed the murderer in twenty-four hours and married my mother twenty-four hours after that. Swept her off her feet. He really had a way with women. Women used to go for that macho stuff. My mother did anyway, they tell me. Of course my parents' marriage was about as happy as life in the Black Hole of Calcutta.

The main reason for all the unhappiness was that Big Jake insisted they live on his earnings despite the fact she had money enough to buy the Principality of Monaco. Big Jake made a good living, but still, what's a good living when you're used to Rolls Royces and wintering in the Bahamas? What a life I had when I was a kid! My mother wanted me to play the violin despite the fact I have no sense of rhythm, a tin ear, and the dexterity of a brine shrimp. I had nine different violin teachers. Mother always blamed them for my lack of skill. But I never wanted to be a musician. When I was about fifteen she finally gave up on the music. She then decided she wanted me to grow up to be a banker. But I wouldn't hear of it. No sir, from the time I was old enough to know what's what, I wanted to be a private eye. And even then, when I was a kid, I was stubborn as hell. When I wanted something, I'd never stop trying to get it until I had it.

Mother said I'd never make it, of course, because I'm not like my father. She fought me like the Boers fought the British. But believe it or not, you don't have to be like Big Jake Mitchell to be good in the business. His style isn't my style. If I ever acted like he did, I would have been broken in half my first year in the business.

My approach to being a private eye was to become a scientific criminologist instead of a cheap thug. In college, I took a lot of chemistry, physics, math, police science, forensic science, and computer programming. I would say I'm a specialist in crime detection. When Big Jake was gunned down in 1982, I was just finishing graduate school. It was a hectic time in my life. I was planning to get married, I had just had an operation on my deviated septum, and I was looking for a house to buy, but I put everything aside and stepped right in and took over his business. . . .

We now have the bare beginnings of the outline of Boyer's life. For an important character such as Boyer, this biographical sketch might be ten to fifty pages long, describing the character from his birth—including family history—up to the beginning of the story.

Now then, why were these *particular* elements of Boyer's biography selected? As noted above, you should choose elements that will have a bearing on the character's emotions and behavior in the story. Boyer was made young-looking because it will cause him to be self-conscious; his appearance may lead other characters not to take him seriously, making it harder for him to do his job. You should always be looking for obstacles for your characters. Boyer's slightness will make it difficult for him to live up to his father's reputation. His mother, who is still living, will be trying to get him to quit the business—yet another obstacle. But he will stubbornly stick to his goals. To compensate Boyer for his lack of physical toughness he is endowed with other abilities: he's smart and studious. His father's death, however, forced him to take over the business before he was ready, which also interrupted his wedding plans. Another problem.

Boyer Bennington Mitchell could have had a completely different background and could have emerged as a completely different character. His father might have been a crooked cop, say, and Boyer might be trying to salvage the family name. Boyer's skills could be of an intuitive rather than scientific nature. His mother could be poor and sick and he could be trying to pay her bills. The way in which Boyer is drawn depends completely on how the author feels about the character. An infinite number of possibilities would work, as long as the end result is a believable, three-dimensional character that will give a good performance in his role in the story.

If you do a thorough job on your biographies you will know your characters well—at least as well as you know your brother, sister, or best friend—before you begin your novel. It is not possible to make a list of all the elements that should be included in these biographical sketches. You should include any detail that affects the motivations and actions of the character. Include anything that influences his relationships, habits, goals, beliefs, superstitions, moral judgments, obsessions, and so on—all the factors that govern choices and behavior. You should know your character's views on politics, religion, friendship, family; his hopes, dreams, hobbies, interests; what he studied in school, which subjects he liked and which he hated. What are his prejudices? What would he hide from his analyst? What would he hide from himself? You should be able to answer any reasonable question anyone might ask you about a character as if that character were someone close to you.

You may complete the biography of your character and still not know all you'd like to know. Say your character found a wallet with $10,000 in it. Would he keep it or return it? If he contracted a fatal disease, would he commit suicide? If he could save one thing from his burning house or apartment, what would that one thing be? If you don't know the answers to such questions, you need to explore your character further before you begin your story.

INTERVIEWING A CHARACTER,
OR, GETTING TO KNOW HIM
THE EASY WAY

If, after you have created your characters, you still do not see them in your mind's eye walking, talking, breathing, perspiring, you might try a little psychoanalysis. Put them on the couch and start asking them questions. Here's how such a session might go:

AUTHOR: What I still don't understand, Boyer, is really why you stay in the business. Your mother, to whom you are very close, does not want you in the business, and your fiancée is demanding you get out of it or the wedding is off.

BOYER: I can tell you this because you're my author, but I wouldn't tell anyone else. I feel like I have to prove something to myself. That's the real reason I stay in the business. Sure, I'm afraid sometimes, but I can't run away. I wouldn't feel like a man if I did.

AUTHOR: I understand—you're competing in a way with your father. Cigarette?

BOYER: You know I don't smoke.

AUTHOR: That's right, I remember. Let's see, I understand you vote Republican.

BOYER: Not true! I'm a registered Republican for family reasons. I'm basically apolitical. I don't vote often, if you want to know the truth. Either I forget or it just doesn't seem to matter a whole lot who's elected. I don't even know much about the issues anyway, and all the candidates look the same to me.

AUTHOR: Tell me about the girl you're going to marry.
BOYER: Sally's a wonderful girl—bright, articulate, sweet.
AUTHOR: Have you ever slept with her?
BOYER: What kind of a question is that?
AUTHOR: It's important, if I'm to understand you, that I know your experiences and attitudes and so on.
BOYER: I've never slept with her.
AUTHOR: Have you ever slept with any girl?
BOYER: Not exactly—there was an almost in college.
AUTHOR: An almost?
BOYER: Yeah, well, *almost.*
AUTHOR: Tell me about it.
BOYER: This will have to be just between you and me. . . .

By the time you've thoroughly interviewed your character, he should have become like a dear friend or a hated enemy. Once you feel that close, you should be confident working with him.

AT THE CHARACTER'S CORE: THE RULING PASSION, AND HOW TO FIND IT

The ruling passion is a character's central motivating force. It is the sum total of all the forces and drives within him. For Boyer Bennington Mitchell, his ruling passion has to do with solving crimes. It is rooted in his family history, in his competitiveness with his macho father, in his wanting to prove his snobby mother wrong, in his drive to overcome his physical limitations by building up his mental capacities. He also has a strong sense of justice and a powerful desire to do a job well. Not just well, let's say he wishes to be an artist at it. Not just an artist, a great artist. Boyer's ruling passion:

To Be the Leonardo da Vinci of Private Eyes.

Will he waver if he meets with discouragement? Not much. Will he be swayed by bribes, threats, hardships? Not a chance. If he is beaten and shot, will he quit? No, because he's out to prove himself; deep inside he will find the strength to go on. It's possible to slow him down, but he will keep coming back to his task. He will solve the crime the author assigns to him or die trying. This kind of determination makes Boyer a strong character. He is well-motivated and strong enough to go the distance despite the numerous obstacles the author is going to place in his path. A worthy protagonist for a dramatic novel indeed.

THE STEADFAST PROTAGONIST, HEARTBEAT OF THE DRAMATIC NOVEL

The protagonist of a dramatic novel should always be determined, well motivated, willful. Here are some examples:

- The old man in Hemingway's *The Old Man and the Sea* has not caught a fish in eighty-four days. He is disgraced. He is impoverished. His very manhood is being derided. He *must* catch a big fish or die trying.
- Michael Corleone in Puzo's *The Godfather* is another example of a worthy protagonist. Michael's father has been shot. His beloved family is under siege. His father's enemies have brought the family to the brink of disaster. Michael Corleone will risk everything to save them.
- Scrooge in Dickens's *A Christmas Carol* is a

protagonist with a negative ruling passion. He's
a passionate miser, unrepentant, ill-humored,
ready at all times to defend his miserliness. And
he does defend it, against all comers, all cheer-
fulness, all happiness—even against the super-
natural. Does that make him a worthy protagonist?
It certainly does.

- How about McMurphy in Kesey's *One Flew
  over the Cuckoo's Nest*? He's going to run things
  his way or else. He refuses to be dominated by
  Big Nurse. He's the Bull Goose Loony, he says.
  He will dominate the ward or die trying.
- Remember Leamas in *The Spy Who Came in
  from the Cold*? He has gone behind the Iron
  Curtain pretending to defect in order to trap an
  East German spy master. He'll do his duty despite
  betrayal, despite disillusionment, despite *everything*, right up to the climactic moment.
- Humbert Humbert, the protagonist of Nabokov's *Lolita*, is a cad, but he has one monumental
  passion, which rules his every waking moment.
  He must have Lolita's love or die.
- Emma Bovary, in Flaubert's *Madame Bovary*,
  is a hopelessly romantic woman stuck in a provincial town, married to a dull country doctor.
  She must find romance despite the risk to her
  reputation. This kind of passion is the stuff of
  which great classics are made.

You need not look far to find other examples in literature.
Think of any character you ever liked and you will find at his
core a definable, strong ruling passion. Look at Defoe's Moll
Flanders and her relentless pursuit of the good life, Tolstoy's
Anna Karenina and her love for Vronski, Melville's Ahab and

his passion to kill Moby Dick. Examine any enduring dramatic novel and you will find central characters with burning passions that rule their every action.

Even though a character is controlled by a burning passion, he acts out of a complexity of motives. Take Boyer Mitchell. He wants to best his dead father. He wants to prove himself to his mother. He has a love of justice. He likes a mystery. He's fascinated by applied science. All of these motives combine to form his ruling passion, to be the Leonardo da Vinci of private eyes. His antagonists will act out of a complexity of motives as well.

STEREOTYPED CHARACTERS
AND HOW TO AVOID THEM

Stereotyped characters are characters that are *too* familiar: the whore with the heart of gold, the Southern sheriff with a slow drawl and a sadistic core, the tough-but-tender private eye. If you watch network television you will see stereotyped characters on nearly every show.

When you say a character is a "John Wayne" type, you mean he is a stereotype of the screen character created by John Wayne. The same is true for the "Woody Allen" type. Readers and audiences like to type characters. It's unavoidable. Whether or not you like to think of your characters as types, your readers will. But there is an enormous difference between fresh characters of a recognizable type and stereotyped characters.

One of the first novels ever written was Defoe's *Moll Flanders*. Moll is a delightful character—lusty, gutsy, full of life. She's an anarchist, a thief, a whore, a bigamist; she commits incest, yet she's honest with herself and has an infectious good humor. What type of character is she? Let's call her a "sympathetic sociopath." A couple of hundred years later another sympathetic sociopath comes along. He's an anarchist—lusty, gutsy, full of life. He's a thief and a liar, and he has an infectious good humor about himself. His name is Zorba the Greek. Moll and Zorba are both of the same "type" but are not stereotypes. The reason? Both have great complexity and depth, and therefore differences abound.

Pierre, in Tolstoy's *War and Peace*, is an innocent in search of meaning as he slogs around in the muck of the Napoleonic Wars. He's indecisive and easily swayed; he attempts understanding through befuddled philosophical speculation. The same is true of Robert Stone's Converse in *Dog Soldiers*, written a hundred years later—except that Converse is slogging around in the muck of the American drug culture of the 1970s. The characters are similar, but they are not Xerox copies. They are similar because traits in both *homo sapiens* and *homo fictus* tend to "clump" together.

If you find a soft-spoken intellectual, an expert on, say, medieval morality plays, he will probably not be a greedy businessman or a shark at three-corner billiards. We expect cute young girls not to be interested in fascist politics. Kindly old grandmothers who like knitting and baking cookies are probably not making bombs in the basement. Expectations about characters in the reader's mind are based on conventions such as these and are signaled by clues authors give about the characters. When you see a black-hatted gun fighter come on the screen in a western, you say to yourself, "Ah, the bad guy." If you see a handsome, boyish, clean-shaven fella, a flower in his holster instead of a gun, a lasso twirling at his side, you say to yourself, "Ah, the good guy."

When *all* the reader's expectations about a character are fulfilled, when there are no contradictions or surprises in the character, you have a stereotyped character. If the old granny is a retired police lieutenant and the bookish intellectual secretly loves boxing, you have a start on breaking the stereotype.

Take, as an example, the stereotype of the tough-guy detective. Say you want to create such a character and you name him Brock Mitchell. He's everything the stereotype calls for: he's resourceful, ruggedly handsome, hard as nails, chews matchsticks, but he's soft as mush on the inside. He likes kittens. He isn't making it well financially, lives alone, has a wry wit and a fondness for rye whiskey. He collects blondes the way a blue serge suit collects lint.

So you've created the perfect stereotype. Philip Marlowe, Jim Rockford, Sam Spade, the Continental Op—this character has had a thousand incarnations. What to do?

Robert B. Parker broke the detective stereotype with Spenser, who loves gourmet cooking and is having a stormy romance with a lady psychologist named Susan Silverman. Donald E. Westlake writing as Richard Stark broke the stereotype by eliminating the soft mushy inside of his character, Parker. So did Mickey Spillane with Mike Hammer. You might make Brock a gambling addict or an ex-priest mourning his loss of faith.

But be warned. You can break the stereotype only if the break is well integrated within the character as a logical outgrowth of his physiology, sociology, and psychology, and not simply contrived by the author to surprise or shock. If Brock Mitchell were, say, sexually involved with a thirteen-year-old girl, you've broken the stereotype all right; you might even be able to make his pedophilia an outgrowth of his physiology, sociology, and psychology; but the reader is likely to find such behavior reprehensible.

You could give him other negative traits that the reader would accept, as long as he's struggling to solve his problem. Say he's a kleptomaniac and is warring with his inclination to steal. The kleptomania might be a result of some boyhood trauma, for example. He might have been severely punished for a theft he never committed. The reader could sympathize with such a character.

The secret of fresh, nonstereotyped characterizations is to combine character traits that the reader would *not* expect to find within the same character. You might draw a character in your novel, Sister Maria of Avignon, who loves comic books. You might find tenderness and compassion where you'd least expect it, say in a Nazi stormtrooper. An artist of the most delicate sensibilities can have a mean streak. There are contradictions to be found in everyone. Readers delight in seeing them in your characters. The trick is, of course, not to go too far. There is no objective standard for knowing what is too far; you have to ask yourself, "Is it believable?"

And like all character traits, contradictions should serve the purpose of the story; they should affect the emotions and the behavior of the character.

CHARACTER MAXIMUM CAPACITY AND THE "WOULD HE REALLY" TEST

Human beings sometimes do foolish things. They misspeak, they forget, they buy when they should sell, they miss opportunities, they're blind to the obvious. In effect, they are not at all times and in all situations operating at their *maximum capacity*. Not so with *homo fictus*.

All of your central characters, both protagonists and antagonists, should at all times be clever and efficient in handling the problems you have presented them. Say your heroine is alone in a spooky house during a thunderstorm. The lights go out. "What's that?"—strange noises are coming from the attic. Groaning and moaning and the clanking of chains. You've seen this scene a million times in cheap horror films. Your heroine finds a candle and lights it. But if she goes anywhere near that attic (as she *always* does in the cheap horror films), you are violating the principle of maximum capacity. No sane and sensible person, no matter how curious, would go up those stairs to the attic. This particular cliché is rather widely known as the "idiot in the attic" motif. Never use it.

The principle of maximum capacity does not require that a character always be at an *absolute* maximum, but at the maximum *within that character's capability*. A weak character in the dramatic sense does not mean weak in the ordinary sense. Your character may be a ninety-pound milquetoast and still be a strong dramatic character—if he knows what he wants and is striving within his capacity to get it. The clever author is always placing obstacles in the path of his characters. It is cheating if the author does not allow a character to use all his capacities to overcome these obstacles. If your character is at his maximum capacity, the reader will never say, "Hey, knucklehead, why don't you just pick up the phone and call the fire department instead of using a garden hose?"

Characters at their maximum capacity will use any and all means available within their particular capacity to achieve their ends. Let's say you have drawn an extremely shy character, Ellen, who is hopelessly in love with a married man who works in the same office. She fantasizes about him. She yearns for a hello from him, which she never gets. His name is Kevin, and he doesn't even know she exists. It is not within Ellen's powers (her capacity) to go up to this man and say, "Hey Kevin, old bone, what do you say we take a tumble in the hay after work tonight?" It is not even within her powers to speak to the man except on business matters, and even then she sputters, demurs, and blushes.

Now suppose you have drawn Ellen from a "real" character you know from the office where you work. Her name is Sue Ellen. Sue Ellen has worked with the "real" Kevin for twenty-two years, and every day of those twenty-two years she has been pining for him without ever saying one word or making a single move. That's real life. Stranger than fiction, as they say. But nothing is happening; there is no drama, no action. The reader grows impatient for something to happen. A story is goal-oriented; it progresses, it develops. *Homo fictus* always operates at his maximum capacity and *it is never within a dramatic character's maximum capacity, when faced with a problem or a challenge, to do nothing unless the lack of action is being played for comedy.*

True, a shy character has a limited range of options for action. In her regular state of mind she is not likely to do anything overt. But there are still a million choices she might make. You, as the storyteller, must select from among all the possible solutions which action she might take within her maximum capacity. Let's say you go into your study and think real hard about all the things your character *could* do. Here are some possibilities:

- She might send a note to Kevin and tell all.
- She might have a friend intervene for her.
- She might telephone Kevin and disguise her voice.
- She might take assertiveness training.
- She might go to charm school.
- She might find out what bar Kevin frequents, then go there in disguise.
- She might find out what church he attends and join the choir to be near him.
- What if she were to meet his wife and befriend her?
- She might get tipsy at a party, find her courage—and make a fool of herself.
- She might manipulate things at the office so she gets appointed his secretary.

- While passing him in the cafeteria she might get flustered and spill her coffee on his new tie.

This list is not exhaustive. You might make up option lists like this whenever a character faces a new dilemma. If the character agonizes, so much the better.

Maximum capacity should always be exhibited but must never be exceeded. In each situation, you must ask yourself whether the contemplated action passes the *would he really* test. Suppose you have characterized Wilfred Frompet as a mild-mannered book dealer. He's bespectacled, fiftyish, retiring, scholarly. Let us say you have him getting into a minor traffic accident. The other driver is a surly foreigner with garlic breath who pushes Wilfred around and knocks his glasses off. You're not sure how Wilfred would respond in this situation. You reread his biography and ponder the possibilities. You want him to be resourceful and determined, so you have him go to the trunk of the car, get out his tire iron, and bludgeon the other driver to death.

What's wrong with that? you ask. It's willful, decisive, and reveals a new facet of his character. The trouble is, such an action flunks the *would he really* test. Such a violent response would be appropriate only in an absurd or satirical piece in which the characters are not intended to be portrayed realistically. Nothing will send a book to the garbage can sooner than a character that causes the reader to say, "Wilfred Frompet would never do a thing like that—at least not the Wilfred Frompet I know."

That is not to say that a character such as Wilfred could not be pushed into such an action if the pressures on him were great enough. In other words, if Wilfred were drafted into the army, he might turn out to be a Sergeant York. In fact, Sergeant York himself refused the draft at first because he was a pacifist.

If you are conscientious in seeking out clever and resourceful alternatives for your characters, your story will prosper. Whenever your characters are faced with decisions that matter, ask yourself these two questions with regard to maximum capacity: "Would he really?" and "What else could he do that is more ingenious, dramatic, surprising, or funny?"

Asking these two questions will help you keep your character acting at his maximum capacity. A character at his maximum capacity always gives the reader a good performance.

But, you say, what if your character has little capacity? Doesn't matter. He will act within that capacity and will surprise and delight just the same. Say you create the character of a business executive who crashes his plane in the desert. He has *no* survival skills; in other words, a low maximum capacity in that situation. His idea of hardship up until this point in his life is having no crushed ice for his vodka martini. His clumsy and ineffectual attempts to dig for water, to milk cacti, to kill lizards, and so on, could make for a damn gripping story, as long as the executive acts at his maximum capacity within the limited range of his skills.

It is also within the maximum capacity of a character to change, to grow, to develop. Characters are not made of concrete. They are living things, and no living thing remains the same. What causes them to change is the fiction writer's magic wand: *conflict*, the subject of the next chapter.

2.

THE THREE GREATEST RULES OF DRAMATIC WRITING: CONFLICT! CONFLICT! CONFLICT!

THE HOW AND WHY OF CONFLICT: BRINGING A CHARACTER TO LIFE

ONE WAY a novelist creates vivid characters is through the use of straightforward narrative:

> Jones was a tall, angular, lanky lumberjack with deep-set, angry eyes. His unkempt, wild, raven hair spilled down over his forehead and the veins in his neck stood out like rope. A scar, jagged and ugly, that seemed to glow in the lantern's yellow light, ran up the side of his face. He was a frightening specter indeed. . . .

With straightforward narrative you may be able to create in the reader's imagination a visual image of a character, but the character will spring to life only when he is put to the test, when he is forced to make a decision and *act*.

Suppose three soldiers on patrol come to a cold stream, which they must cross. It's November and there's a chill wind. Not a good day to go wading. The sergeant grants them a ten-minute rest. One soldier wades into the stream and takes his rest on the other side, preferring to get it over with. Another soldier chooses to spend his rest period walking upstream to a shallower spot, foregoing the rest, but avoiding at least some of the cold water. The sergeant rests on the near side of the stream and waits until the end of the rest period to cross.

The choices these men have made are not momentous, but the way they each handle the problem characterizes them. One prefers to get unpleasantness over with, one will go out of his way to avoid unpleasantness, and the third will put off unpleasantness as long as possible. A character's response to obstacles, barriers, and conflict individualizes him, proves his characterization, and makes him real and distinct in the reader's mind.

Consider the following scene, which has been carefully constructed to put you to sleep:

"Good morning," he said sleepily.

"Good morning," she said.

"Breakfast ready?"

"No. What would you like?"

He considered. "How about ham and eggs?"

"Okay," she said, agreeably. "How do you want your eggs?"

"Sunny-side up."

"Okey-dokey. Toast? I've got some honey wheat bread. Makes wonderful toast."

"I'll give it a try."

"Okey-dokey. How do you like your toast?"

"Golden brown."

"Butter?"

"Hmmmm—okay."

"Jam?"

"Fine."

He sat down and read the paper while she made the breakfast.

"Anything in the paper?" she asked as she worked.

"The Red Sox lost a doubleheader last night."

"Too bad."

"Now they're eight games out of first place."

"Terrible. What are you going to do today?"

"I don't know, haven't thought about it. How about you?"

"The grass needs cutting."

"I'll do it."

"After you cut the grass, let's go to the park, have a picnic lunch."

"Okay. . . ."

What do you feel as you read the scene? Boredom, no doubt. The scene does seem vaguely realistic, but the characters are flat, dull, and lifeless because there is no *conflict*. We know very little about these characters, except perhaps that they are agreeable, because they have done nothing to show their colors. They have not shown us through their actions what they are inside. They are flat, dull, and lifeless because all they do is talk. They don't want anything. They are having a conversation, not dialogue. Most readers will not tolerate such "talkiness" very long. If there are no conflicts on the horizon, the reader will abandon the story. In *The Craft of Fiction* (1977), William C. Knott puts it this way:

"The most elaborate plot in the world is useless without the tension and excitement that conflict imports to it."

Conflict is the collision of characters' desires with resistance —from nature, from other characters, from the spirit world, from outer space, from another dimension, from within themselves, from anywhere. We see *who* the characters are by the way they respond to such resistance; conflict highlights and exposes them. Character, not action, is what interests readers most. It is character that makes action meaningful. Story is struggle. *How* a character struggles reveals *who* he is.

Consider the following scene, in which the two characters are not only speaking to one another, but are also in conflict:

"A merry Christmas, uncle! God save you!" cried a cheerful voice.

"Bah!" said Scrooge. "Humbug!"

"Christmas humbug, uncle!" said Scrooge's nephew. "You don't mean that, I'm sure."

"I do," said Scrooge. "Merry Christmas indeed! What right have you to be merry? What reason have you to be merry? You're poor enough."

"Come then," returned the nephew gaily. "What right have you to be dismal? What reason have you to be morose? You're rich enough."

"Bah!" Scrooge said again. "Humbug!"

"Don't be cross, uncle!" said the nephew.

"What else can I be," returned the uncle, "when I live in such a world of fools as this? Merry Christmas! Out upon merry Christmas! What's Christmas-time to you but a time for paying bills without money; a time for finding yourself a year older, and not an hour richer; a time for balancing your books and having every item in 'em through a round dozen of months pre-

hapless Wimpy. There can pnflict will remain in
without evenly matched cobonded together by love
any challenge to Popeye; hot simply walk away.
sourcefulness and skills or hi
could best Wimpy without fill remain in conflict
quately tested only when he or divorce. They are
The creators of this cartoomiage, love, and duty.
who pit Muhammad Ali ag,
lowing the principle called in, if there is conflict,
(1983), Raymond Hull expla t because neither can
"M + G + O = C. Main te cell is bonding them
= Conflict." le.
Good opposition requires)ple in a lifeboat: since
the protagonist's attempts to are in a crucible.
force and cunning as the pr nnot get away from his
Good opposition does no much he hates him.
Dudley Do-Right who is pur ucible.
or that your antagonist be
ruthless, and cruel. Dudley mples:
is equally pure, noble, and
better if he is. 'lew over the Cuckoo's
Good opposition does no mental hospital, is de-
lain. The antagonist may kGoose Loony." He can-
This does not mean that vill ere by order of the court;
They have their place. Th crushed. Big Nurse is
required for good opposition. She's boss of the ward
What is required for g succeed in challenging
rounded, nonstereotyped ch g in total control of the
Say you've decided to tel rs in her life. McMurphy
Allgood, struggling against t ed together; the mental
pany. The chief sexist is the
you create Hiram as a dim-w ld Man and the Sea has
ing that a "woman's place i He can't let go because
h to prove his manhood,

and the fish can't get free because of the hook in its mouth. They are bonded in a death struggle; it is their crucible.

- The Corleones' enemies in *The Godfather* have set out to take much of the Corleone family's power. Michael Corleone must stop them or be smashed. Neither side can run away; neither side can achieve a quick victory. Both must fight the war to the end. Their duty to their respective families is their crucible.
- In *Madame Bovary*, Emma is married to a man she detests. In her day, divorce is impossible. She is chained to him. Their marriage is their crucible.
- In *Lolita*, Humbert Humbert loves Lolita. She is a child and must stay with him because she has nowhere else to go. His love and her dependency form their crucible.

INNER CONFLICT AND THE NECESSITY THEREOF

When a character's will collides with an obstacle that occurs *within* the character himself, as when duty collides with fear, love with guilt, ambition with conscience, and so on, you have inner conflict. Characters suffer inner conflicts just as real people do. Real people often vacillate. Wracked by indecision, they have guilt pangs, fears, misgivings, doubts, second thoughts, and the like. These are all manifestations of inner conflict. Inner conflicts make characters not only interesting but truly memorable to the reader. Whenever a reader experiences profound empathy with a character, it is because the character is in the throes of intense inner conflict. A character may be in the most pathetic straits in the history of literature, but if he has no inner conflict, the only emotional response the writer can expect from the reader is pity.

If Humbert Humbert had no inner conflict over his lusting after a nymphet, the reader would loathe him.

The old man has great sympathy for the fish and feels remorse over killing it. If he didn't, we'd have an adventure yarn, hardly worth reading.

Leamas, behind the Iron Curtain, comes to the realization that the machinations of his government are just as bad as those of the communists. His inner conflict is so great that he resolves it by accepting death.

Without Madame Bovary's inner conflict, Flaubert's novel would be no more worth reading than a Harlequin Romance. Who cares if a housewife has a fling?

Michael Corleone is a man of conscience, but he loves his family and feels compelled to come to their aid in times of trouble. How tortured is his soul!

If your characters have no inner conflicts, your work will be a melodrama. Inner conflict confirms that the characters are involved, that something is at risk for them.

Say you're planning to write a story about a man who wants to marry a woman. He woos her; she resists. It is difficult, but she finally says yes. That's the core of the story. The insistence (wooing) and resistance make it dramatic, but it is not as dramatic as it could be. This situation would tend towards melodrama because the central characters have no inner conflicts. So you start brainstorming for ideas to build inner conflict into your characters. You ask yourself, what if he is Zen Buddhist and takes his religion seriously, but she is not Zen, and his parents and his Zen community oppose the marriage? Now he has inner conflict over going against his family's wishes. She loves him but has inner conflict over coming between him and his family. Then you would have the makings of a truly dramatic novel.

Inner conflict need not arise only over religion, of course. It might arise over anything: cultural or racial differences, class, ethnic background, temptations, sexual desires or fantasies, omissions of duty, patriotism, loyalty, laziness—anything a character might feel strongly about.

If a wicked monster threatens a man's family and the man kills the monster, he will not suffer remorse, pangs of guilt, doubts, or misgivings. When Godzilla is eating Tokyo, it is okay to kill Godzilla. There are no moral choices to be made; characters either run away or stand and fight. Either is an acceptable moral choice. No one is called chicken for running away from Godzilla. The battle against Godzilla might make a good action yarn for the Sunday comics, but it is not suitable material for a dramatic novel. No inner conflict.

To have inner conflict, the opposing forces need not be great or the issues earth-shaking. They need only be great in the minds of the characters involved. One man may torture himself over having stolen a dime, while another steals a million bucks and doesn't lose a wink of sleep. There is more inherent drama in the story of the man who steals the dime if the theft means the loss of his integrity, honor, self-esteem, and the like, than in the story of the million-dollar thief who is indifferent to the moral consequences of his actions.

Exploiting the inner conflicts of your characters is a tricky business. If your protagonist is called upon to go to war, make certain he is reluctant to do so for a powerful reason. He might be a pacifist; he might be a coward; he might be opposed to his country's policies. If your protagonist is to fall in love with an Irish Catholic, make him an English Protestant. If you're going to test a man's patriotism, be sure patriotism matters to him. This is called "impaling your character on the horns of a dilemma."

You have impaled your character on the horns of a dilemma whenever your character *must have* or *must do* something—for very powerful and convincing reasons—and yet *can't have* or *can't do* that something for equally powerful and compelling reasons. You'll know your character is impaled when he's being ripped apart by equally powerful forces pulling in opposite directions.

Say a young man feels compelled to kill his mother's new husband to avenge his father's death, yet he is intensely moral and opposed to killing. Moreover, he has doubts that his stepfather is guilty, despite the fact that his father's ghost tells him his stepfather is the murderer. A character impaled on the horns of such a dilemma could be the star of a gripping drama. Of course, such a drama has already been written. It was called *Hamlet.*

PATTERNS OF DRAMATIC CONFLICT: STATIC, JUMPING, AND SLOWLY RISING

In *Technique of the Drama* (1894), Gustav Freytag wrote, "What drama presents is a struggle, which, with strong perturbations of the soul [inner conflict], the hero wages against opposing forces." The struggle is the action of a drama. Freytag pointed out that "action rises to the point of the climax, and then falls away." He called the climax "the most important place of the structure."

To Lajos Egri, the struggle, the action, is "conflict." Conflict which fails to rise he calls "static." Conflict which rises too quickly he calls "jumping." What Freytag called "rising action," Egri calls "slowly rising conflict," which is what the dramatist wants. But the question for the writer is how do you tell whether your conflict is static, jumping, or slowly rising?

Static conflict is any kind of dramatic conflict that is unchanging. Characters firing artillery barrages at each other are engaged in intense conflict, but it remains at the same level. It is therefore static. Bickering and nagging are static forms of conflict. Two children yelling, "Yes you will!—No I won't!—Yes you will!—No I won't!" are engaged in static conflict.

When the conflicts become static, a novel runs aground on a sandbar. Characters in the midst of static conflict, Egri points out, stop developing. The shy character remains shy, the brave character stays brave; the weak remain weak, the strong stay strong. Nothing bores a reader as much as static conflict except no conflict at all.

Jumping conflict leaps from one level of intensity to another without adequate motivation or transitional stages. A character, say, might react with hatred and vehemence when annoyance would be more appropriate. Jumping conflict is commonly seen in cheap melodramas. Characters are tender and loving one moment, raging the next, then forgiving, and on and on. The reader gets dizzy. It's possible, of course, to have an emergency in which the characters jump from one emotional state to another quickly. If Godzilla steps on your character's living room unexpectedly, the conflict might jump considerably. Jumping conflict is a fault when the jump—the rapid change in a character's emotional state—is not justified by the situation.

In the best dramatic novels, the conflicts rise slowly. Conflict *proves* character. *Slowly rising conflict* will reveal more facets of character than jumping or static conflict because the characters will react differently at each stage of the conflict. As the character responds to a rising conflict, he changes, showing all of his colors.

In a slowly rising conflict, a character will go through several emotional stages, say, from annoyance to peevishness, to mild anger, to intense anger, to insane anger. In a jumping conflict, he'd go from annoyance to insane anger. In a static conflict, he'd stay at one level, say intense anger, throughout the scene. By the climax of a slowly rising conflict the character is fully revealed because the reader has seen him acting and reacting at each emotional level.

The art of writing the dramatic novel is the art of holding the reader gripped in a slowly rising conflict. The secret of slowly rising conflict, Egri says, is to think of conflict in terms of attacks and counterattacks, as if the protagonist and antagonist were strategists conducting a war. Here's an example:

"You don't believe in me," observed the Ghost [Explains the obvious; he's not attacking yet, he's simply stating his position.]

"I don't," said Scrooge. [A statement of his position.]

"What evidence would you have of my reality beyond that of your own senses?" [Low-level attack.]

"I don't know," said Scrooge. [Low-level defense. So far, they're merely probing each other.]

"Why do you doubt your senses?" [Increased attack.]

"Because," said Scrooge, "a little thing affects them. A slight disorder of the stomach makes them cheats. You may be an undigested bit of beef, a blot of mustard, a crumb of cheese, a fragment of underdone potato. [Defense.] There's more of gravy than of grave about you, whatever you are! [Counterattack.] You see this toothpick?" said Scrooge. [Setting up for an attack.]

"I do," replied the Ghost. [Getting ready a defense by feigning reasonableness.]

"You are not looking at it," said Scrooge. [Attack.]

"But I see it," said the Ghost, "notwithstanding." [Defense.]

"Well!" returned Scrooge, "I have but to swallow this, and be for the rest of my days persecuted by a legion of goblins, all of my own creation. Humbug I tell you; humbug!" [A full broadside, a rise in the conflict.]

At this point the spirit raised a frightful cry, and shook his chain with such a dismal and appalling noise [a massive counterattack], that Scrooge held on tight to his chair, to save himself from falling in a swoon. [Retreat]. But how much greater was his horror when, the phantom taking off the bandage round his head, as if it were too warm to wear indoors, his lower jaw dropped down upon his breast! [Massive attack, a frontal assault.]

Scrooge fell upon his knees and clasped his hands before his face. [Full retreat.] "Mercy!" he said. "Dreadful apparition, why do you trouble me?" [New tactic, attack.]

"Man of the worldly mind!" replied the Ghost, "do you believe in me or not?" [Counterattack.]

"I do," said Scrooge. [Surrender.]

A novice writer might have had Scrooge on his knees at the first sight of the Ghost. Dickens exploited the conflict for its full potential through a rising conflict.

Now then, how might you approach the creation of your novel to make sure you have a rising conflict? First, plan your novel with rising conflict always in mind. Your characters should be facing ever-increasing obstacles; their problems should be multiplying; pressures on them should always be growing.

Say your protagonist's problem is that he's been fired from his job. At first it's a minor problem, but as his bills come due and he begins to hide his car so it won't be repossessed, the pressure on him to find a job grows more intense. Then his wife wants to leave him, the bank threatens to foreclose on his mortgage, and his best friend—his dog—has an allergic reaction to the cheap dog food he's being forced to eat. . . .

And so it goes. Your hero is engaged in a rising conflict, a developing crisis.

The conflict can rise only if there is character development. As the conflict rises, the character changes. When Scrooge in the scene above first meets the Ghost, he is cool; he looks the Ghost in the eye and says, "You're only in my imagination." Then the Ghost raises a "frightful cry" and takes off his bandages so that his "lower jaw dropped down upon his breast." Scrooge loses his cool; he falls on his knees and cries, "Mercy!" This is a rise in the action. Would Scrooge fall on his knees and make such a cry if he had not lost his cool? If he had not changed? Nope.

The same would be true with your character who has lost his job. If he's cool when he loses it, and cool when his car is repossessed, and cool when his dog gets sick, and cool when his wife leaves him, and cool when he's losing his house, then there is no rising conflict. There is simply a cool character withstanding the slings and arrows of outrageous fortune, and the reader would soon get bored with that. Unless it were being played for comedy.

To ensure that you have a rising conflict, look at your character's emotional level at the beginning of the scene and at the end of the scene. There should be a step-by-step change in the character from, say, cool to fearful, spiteful to forgiving, cruel to compassionate, or the like, in every scene. If there is conflict but no change, you have a static conflict. If the characters change in the scene but do not progress steadily, you may have a jumping conflict. However, if the characters change emotionally a little at a time as a result of the conflict, you know the conflict is rising slowly, as it should.

GENRES,
THE PIGEONHOLES
OF LITERATURE

In every dramatic story there is a "core" conflict. If you read a story and someone later asks you what it was about, the high-speed computer in your cranium will do a quick analysis of all the conflicts in the story, seek out the core conflict from the peripheral conflicts, and—voila!—your answer. It's about a ship accident, you'll say. The sinking of the Titanic.

- The core conflict in *The Old Man and the Sea* is the death struggle between the old man and the big fish.
- The core conflict in *The Spy Who Came in from the Cold* is between Leamas and his East German interrogators.
- The core conflict of *A Christmas Carol* is between Scrooge and the spirits.
- In *Lolita*, the core conflict is between Humbert Humbert and Lolita.
- In *The Godfather*, the core conflict is between the Corleones and the other New York Mafia families.
- In Madame Bovary, Emma is in conflict with her strait-laced society; that conflict is at the core of the novel.
- McMurphy's conflict with Big Nurse is at the core of *One Flew over the Cuckoo's Nest*.

In each of these novels there are many other conflicts. Scrooge is in conflict with his nephew, his clerk, and the gentlemen who come to ask him for money. McMurphy is in conflict not only with Big Nurse, but with the other patients on the ward and the other members of the staff. Leamas is in conflict with his girlfriend and his superiors. The Corleones are involved in all kinds of nefarious activities which generate dozens of conflicts. Emma Bovary has problems with her husband Charles as well as with her lovers.

So stories may and often do contain the threads of many developing conflicts. A character may be involved in a romance while he's plotting the overthrow of the king. A character might be going through a divorce while she's trying to get a decent job. But in a dramatic novel, there will always be an easily identifiable core conflict. The core conflict is what theorists such as Raymond Hull write about when they describe, as Hull does in *How to Write a Play*, the types of conflict as "man against nature," "man against man," "man against society," "man against himself," "man against fate," and so on.

Although the core conflict will determine what the novel is about, it does not necessarily determine its genre. Genre refers to a book's literary classification based on formulas, rules, and marketing conventions in the book trade. Books are marketed as "literary," "mainstream," "mysteries," "science fiction," and so on. Like it or not, as a novelist you will have to abide by these formulas, rules, and conventions.

Americans are prejudiced in favor of being creative and often find repugnant the very idea of writing in restrictive genres. Unfortunately, it is unavoidable. The reason: making judgments based on type (in this case, genre) is the way the human psyche works.

Put yourself in the place of the reader for a moment. You have been given a book for your birthday titled *The Fruitcake* by James N. Frey. Your brother-in-law, who gave you the book, lost the cover (the boob!) so you have no jacket copy to tell you what this book might be. The title might mean it's a cookbook. A fruitcake is also a crazy person. You open the book. It says, "The Fruitcake" and right underneath that is written, "A novel."

You have just made your first judgment as to type. Ah, good, it's fiction.

The dedication reads: "To my loving wife, Elizabeth, who's had to live with the fruitcake and put up with all his nuttiness." You now make your second judgment as to type. Upon reading the dedication you make a guess that, because the author has identified himself as the fruitcake, it must be an autobiographical novel about a nut.

It sounds like something Kurt Vonnegut would write and you like Kurt Vonnegut, so you say to yourself, hmmm, might be good. You have an expectation based on type. You read the next page. There's a quote from Shakespeare: "There's small choice in rotten apples." Okay, you say, this is a comedy. Exactly what kind you don't know, but if it starts with a quote like that it must be a comedy.

Chapter 1 is the account of the protagonist/narrator, identified as the author himself, having a rollicking good time in high school in Syracuse, New York, in the mid-fifties, getting drunk, making love to a giggly girl in the back seat of a '49 Merc, getting beat up by the defensive end on the football team. Fun stuff like that. The tone is light, the dialogue breezy and witty; you decide it's a *Catcher in the Rye* kind of book, but funnier. You've pinned down the type, the genre. You've made up your mind based on the title, the dedication, the quote from Shakespeare, and the contents of chapter 1.

Chapter 2 begins with the giggly girl introduced in chapter 1 found brutally murdered, and Jimmy, the breezy narrator, accused of the crime. The victim was pregnant with Jimmy's baby, it's discovered. You realize suddenly you were wrong in your guess as to genre. This novel now seems deadly serious. Your hero sets out to find the real killer. Based on your identification of the core conflict as the struggle to find the killer, you now classify the book as a murder mystery, your fourth guess as to type. Your perception of the book's genre has now changed substantially—from comedy to murder mystery.

Chapter 3 begins with Jimmy encountering aliens. These folks are from planet K-74, called *The Fruitcake*, way out in the galaxy; they had left the girl on Earth some years before and are now returning to pick her up. The extraterrestrials are bunglers, and the book turns into a bizarre farce where one of the extraterrestrials is put on trial for the murder of the girl. . . .

So it goes.

You will notice that as the reader reads, he is making decisions along the way based on his expectation of the author's intentions as to type; it is the author's intention, perceived by the reader, that determines the genre. As you can see from the farce called *The Fruitcake*, it doesn't matter if there is such a type of book as a "comedy/sex romp/murder mystery/sci-fi/courtroom drama." The reader adjusts his notion of genre as he reads, but there are some adjustments he will not make. Most readers want to be able to guess immediately what the genre is—from the cover and jacket blurb if possible. If you fool them too much, they will abandon your novel. You lose. *The Fruitcake*, sadly, would be called a "zany" novel, and would have a very limited audience.

Some genres succeed in the marketplace better than others, since readers know by past experience, say, that they prefer murder mysteries to surreal fantasies. Simple as that. Easily identifiable types of fiction—genres—are easier to sell. Editors know what readers like. At least they like to tell themselves that they know. Few editors want to take a chance by breaking convention. Therefore, the conventions of genre become more and more rigid as the years go by, until they are so rigid that the writer is in a straitjacket. When this happens, you have formula fiction, written under very strict guidelines. Romance novels have for the most part become formula fiction.

No matter what tradition you are writing in, literary, mainstream, or one of the many other categories—science fiction, romance, mystery, gothic, fantasy, and so on—you will have to know the conventions, rules, and formulas of those types or you might just as well forget about being a published novelist.

How do you learn what the rules are? You go to the library and check out an armful of the type of book you'd like to write, and you read like a maniac. Sorry, but there are no shortcuts. If you don't read deeply in the type of fiction you want to write, you are doomed to failure. You must be steeped in the traditions, conventions, and pigeonholes—the genres.

Once you know the genre, you'll know what premises are provable within that genre. Premise? What's that? you ask. If you think of conflict as the gunpowder of storytelling, premise is the cannon.

It is also the subject of chapter 3.

3.

THE TYRANNY OF THE PREMISE, OR, WRITING A STORY WITHOUT A PREMISE IS LIKE ROWING A BOAT WITHOUT OARS

WHAT'S A PREMISE?

- Think of a premise as the love in a marriage.
- Think of a premise as the abracadabra that puts the rabbit into the hat.
- Think of a premise as the steel in reinforced concrete.
- Think of a premise as the $E = mc^2$ of novel writing.

It is all of the above and more.

- It is the reason you are writing what you are writing.

- It is the point you have to prove.
- It is the *raison d'être* of your novel.
- It is the core, the heart, the center, the soul of your expression.

Still don't get it? Read on.

ORGANIC UNITY AND HOW IT'S ACHIEVED

Mary Burchard Orvis, in *The Art of Writing Fiction* (1948), states:

> All good fiction has form, no matter how modern or surrealistic. Indeed, the particular value of fiction over raw experience is that it imposes a pattern or a meaning upon life. Life is frustrating, chaotic, illogical, fantastic, and, more often than not, apparently meaningless; full of useless suffering, pain, tragedy. Yet man, as a rational and idealistic creature, craves order, plan, and satisfaction of individual potentialities. He may turn to religion, philosophy, poetry, or fiction for his answer to the riddle of life. If he turns to fiction, he wants some sort of organization, meaning, and pattern. . . .

Aristotle was well aware of the need to impose organization on fiction. In *The Poetics*, he explains "unity of action," stating that stories should be "complete and whole in themselves, with a beginning, a middle, and an end . . . with all the organic unity of a living creature."

Theorists ever since have been trying to find the underlying principle that would produce such a unity. This principle could then be used as a critical tool to determine which elements of a story, which characters, incidents, complications, developments, values, and so on belong in the story as part of its organic unity, and which do not.

For example, in *Technique of the Drama*, Gustav Freytag attempts to arrive at the principle underlying organic unity. After discussing in his somewhat florid style how story elements are combined in the "soul of the poet," he explains how these elements are molded and changed:

> This transformation goes on to such an extent that the main element, vividly perceived, and comprehended in its entrancing, soul-stirring or terrifying significance, is separated from all that casually accompanies it, and with single supplementary, invented elements, is brought into a unifying relation of cause and effect. The new unit which thus arises is the *Idea* of the Drama. This is the center toward which further independent inventions are directed, like rays. This idea works with a power similar to the secret power of crystallization. . . .

Freytag's notion of the *Idea* of the Drama was a good attempt at describing the principle underlying unity of action.

Moses L. Malevinsky, however, in *The Science of Playwriting*, disagrees with Freytag's contention that the underlying principle was an "Idea" at all. He writes: "It is our contention the point of origin or initiative of a play is a basic emotion, or an element in or of a basic emotion . . . ."

William Foster-Harris, in his widely read *The Basic Formulas of Fiction* (1944), has yet another notion. He claims the underlying principle is a "solved illustration of a problem of moral arithmetic," such as *Pride + Love = Happiness*. Many beginning writers have found his formulas extremely useful in approaching the writing of a story.

Perhaps the most useful way of expressing the underlying principle is as a syllogism possibly first proposed by W. T. Price in *The Analysis of Play Construction and Dramatic Principle* (1908). He claimed that the underlying principle could best be expressed as a "proposition" which he defined as "the brief, logical statement or syllogism of that which has to be demonstrated by the complete action of the play."

Lajos Egri calls this syllogism a "premise" or "purpose," which he says is another name for "theme, root idea, central idea, goal, aim, driving force, subject, plan, plot, or basic emotion." Egri chooses to call it a *premise* "because it contains all the elements the other words try to express and because it is less subject to misinterpretation."

Egri was talking about playwriting, but this is also true if you're trying to write a damn good novel.

PREMISE DEFINED

If you wished to make an argument, say, that "dogs make better pets than cats," how would you go about proving it? You would argue that dogs are friendlier, more trainable, more likeable, more agreeable, and so on. You would include all the good things you can think of about dogs and all the bad things about cats. Even if you knew any good things about cats, you would exclude them, because it would be contrary to your argument. The premise of an argument is the statement of the *conclusion* that will be reached through the argument. Each part of the argument must contribute to the premise if the argument is to be a good one.

If you were to write a polemical (argumentative) nonfiction book, you would proceed in much the same way as if you were making a simple argument. Your book would be, in effect, a lengthy argument. You would have a premise to prove; that premise would be your conclusion. Say you wished to write a nonfiction book which argues that "white-collar crime pays." You would not have a chapter detailing the lengthy prison sentences of famous white-collar criminals. You couldn't. That would be counter to your premise. You would instead point out the hundreds of white-collar criminals who have gone off to Brazil and are living in the lap of luxury on their ill-gotten gains.

Take a look at any good polemical nonfiction book; you can easily find the author's premise. A book titled *Robert E. Lee, Hero of the Confederacy* will tell you all about Lee and the Civil War; it will not have a chapter on picking roses in Tibet. A book about saving wildlife will not have an appendix on poker playing. The premise holds the author to his subject.

In a nonfiction book the author's premise is a "universal" truth. The premise might be: "war is bad," "pesticides are beneficial," "Millard Fillmore was a great president." It is "universal" because it is always and everywhere provable in the same way the author has proved it. If the reader buys the argument, he is persuaded he now holds a truth, even if another authority would attempt to persuade the reader otherwise. In support of the premise, the nonfiction writer offers evidence that is testable and arguable in the "real" universe.

The premise of a work of fiction, however, is *not* provable and arguable in the "real" world. The reason: the premise of a work of fiction is *not* a universal truth. In a novel the premise is true *only* for the particular situation of that novel.

You may, for example, wish to prove in your novel that "premarital sex leads to disaster." You invent two characters, Sam and Mary, who have premarital sex, as a result of which bad things befall them. Sam, because of guilt, becomes despondent and turns to drink. He loses his job and ends up a derelict. Mary, having lost her virtue, is shunned by her family. She is deserted by Sam. In the end she commits suicide. You have proved your premise, not in the "real" universe, but in the fictional world of the novel. Premarital sex has led to disaster. This premise is not a universal truth—it is not true for all couples—but it is true for Sam and Mary.

Your next novel might have as its premise: "premarital sex leads to bliss." In this novel, Harry and Beth have a little fun behind the barn and their dull lives as a tractor driver and a milkmaid are transformed: they are invigorated, leave the farm, and find rewarding careers in the city. As it is not true that premarital sex leads to bliss for everyone, this is not a universal truth, but it is true for Harry and Beth within the fictional world you have created.

The premise of a story is simply *a statement of what happens to the characters as a result of the core conflict in the story.* Consider these examples:

- In *The Godfather*, Puzo shows us a reluctant son becoming a Mafia don because he loves and respects the family. The premise: "family loyalty leads to a life of crime." Puzo proved it well.
- In *The Old Man and the Sea*, Hemingway sets out to prove the premise that "courage leads to redemption." In the case of the old man it does.
- Dickens, in *A Christmas Carol*, shows us a miserly old man who is confronted with his misdeeds by the spirits of Christmas, and who is transformed into a kind of Santa Claus. The premise: "forced self-examination leads to generosity."
- Le Carre, in *The Spy Who Came in from the Cold*, shows us that even the greatest of spies can be demoralized by the duplicity of his own government. The premise: "realization leads to suicide."

- Kesey's *One Flew over the Cuckoo's Nest* proves the premise that "even the most determined and ruthless psychiatric establishment cannot crush the human spirit."
- Nabokov's *Lolita* proves that "great love leads to death." It does in Humbert Humbert's case.
- Flaubert knew premise well. *Madame Bovary* proves that "illicit love leads to death."

Does every dramatic story have a premise? Yes. One and only one premise? Yes. You can't ride two bicycles at the same time and you can't prove two premises at the same time. What if Dickens in *A Christmas Carol* were also trying to prove that "crime doesn't pay" along with his premise that "forced self-examination leads to generosity"? He'd have Scrooge exposed as a crook and punished. Wouldn't work, would it? What if Kesey wished to prove that "love conquers all," in addition to his premise "even the most determined and ruthless psychiatric establishment cannot crush the human spirit"? He'd really have a cuckoo's nest. How could he make his statement about the uncrushable nature of the human spirit at the same time? He clearly couldn't.

Why a story can have only one premise is self-evident once you understand the nature of premise. In fiction, the premise is the conclusion of a fictive argument. You cannot prove two different premises in a nonfiction argument; the same is true for a fictive argument. Say the character ends up dead. How did it happen? He ended up dead because he tried to rob the bank. He tried to rob the bank because he needed money. He needed money because he wanted to elope. He wanted to elope because he was madly in love. Therefore, his being madly in love is what got him killed; "great love leads to death" is the premise.

If the end of the story does not have a cause-and-effect relationship with what came before, it is not a dramatic story. Aristotle said, "Of simple plots and actions the episodic are the worst. I call a plot episodic when there is neither probability nor necessity in the sequence of its episodes." In other words, no cause-and-effect relationship. Without this relationship, incidents do not build to a climax. By definition, then, a dramatic story can have only one premise because it can have only one climax. At the climax the core conflict is resolved. To say the core conflict is resolved is simply another way of saying the premise is proved.

A novel, of course, *may* be made up of more than one story. *The Old Man and the Sea* is a single story. So is *Madame Bovary*. So is *One Flew over the Cuckoo's Nest*. But Irwin Shaw's *Rich Man, Poor Man* is made up of many stories. The stories are related to one another because they all happen to members of the Jordache family. The novel as a whole has no premise, only a framework, but each story within the framework has its own premise. These are concurrent separate stories, or subplots, which are woven into the main story. These stories have premises of their own like any other.

PREMISES THAT WORK, AND THOSE THAT DON'T

In chapter 1 a detective story was discussed. It involved a young detective named Boyer Bennington Mitchell who was out to prove himself the equal of his hard-boiled father. Boyer was going to solve a crime perpetrated by a woman who murdered her husband to spare her family the disgrace of his being exposed as a dope dealer. What is the premise of this story? How about: "the truth wills out"?

Well? The murderess gets caught in the end and her crime is exposed, right? The truth does will out. Isn't that a nifty premise? No, it isn't. It's much too vague. It would serve for every detective novel ever written. A premise must be specific to the story. In this case, the murderess kills to avoid disgrace, gets caught, and is disgraced. The premise, therefore, is: "desire to avoid disgrace brings disaster and disgrace upon herself and the ones she hoped to protect."

Her desire to maintain her status, in fact, is a burning passion. It leads her to kill. The premise could be put more succinctly as "passion for status leads to disgrace."

Here are some such premises that are so generalized that they are worthless:

- Strangers are not trustworthy.
- Poverty is bad.
- War kills people.
- Life is good.
- Existence leads to death.
- Life is too short.

Most of the above premises can be made viable as follows:

- Trust (of a stranger) leads to disillusionment.
- Unbridled greed (caused by being brought up in poverty) leads to alienation.
- War brutalizes even the most noble.
- Love leads to happiness.
- "Existence leads to death" cannot be made into a viable premise. It's simply a statement that every living thing dies.
- "Life is too short" also cannot be made into a viable premise. It might serve as a story's moral, but not its premise.

FINDING YOUR PREMISE

The germinal idea for a story may be anything. A feeling. An image. A vague recollection of a heartthrob you almost danced with at your high-school prom twenty years ago. Or it might be a person you once met on a bus, or your old Uncle Wilmont who drank too much. It might be a "what if." What if a Martian were elected president? What if a bag lady found a million bucks? What if a great swimmer became a paraplegic? A germinal idea might be nothing more than a vague feeling that a story can be made out of a character, a situation, a notion. You want to write a story, so you pick the germinal idea you like best. Say it's Uncle Wilmont. That's the first step. Next, you sit down with pen and paper and begin looking for your story.

William C. Knott, in *The Craft of Fiction*, advises that you start not with a premise (which he calls a theme), but rather with characters "who demand to be whatever life you can create for them on the printed page. It is the characters who must galvanize you to write, insisting that you tell their story."

So you start with Uncle Wilmont, even though you may not know exactly what it is you want to say about him or have him do. All you know is that Uncle Wilmont is an interesting guy. He collects bugs. He smokes strong-smelling tobacco. He tells funny jokes. He argues loudly with his wife. He's an old socialist whose passions never cooled. Now how do you use this fascinating character in a story? You picture him in your mind and think real hard, but nothing happens. No story emerges, no matter how much you think. You're stuck. Where's the story? Something has to happen to Uncle Wilmont. What you're looking for, of course, is a dilemma. To set a forest on fire, you light a match. To set a character on fire, you put him in conflict.

One thing that has always struck you about Uncle Wilmont is that he's a skinflint. He loves money. What if, say, a swindler came by and wanted him to buy some swampland in Florida? Would he go for it? He might. Uncle Wilmont is very greedy. You decide to start a rough draft and see what happens. You don't have a premise yet, but you have the first part: "greed leads to—?"

Your next step is to think about what might happen in the end. You would like to see Uncle Wilmont taught a lesson, but that wouldn't seem real. Uncle Wilmont has always been greedy and he has never had to pay. No, somehow Uncle Wilmont would turn the situation to his advantage. He would end up winning. What does he win? Wealth? Spirituality? Love? You want to make this story something special. Say he does get swindled. He might make a big stink. He might get his picture in the paper. *Time* Magazine might do an article on him. Uncle Wilmont would be great in an interview. Donahue might have him on. The country might find him refreshing. He might, in pursuit of his greed, find fame. Your premise: "greed leads to fame."

There is no formula for finding a premise. You simply start with a character or a situation, give the protagonist a dilemma, and then meditate on how it might go. Let your imagination run. The possibilities are usually endless.

Okay, say you finish that story and want to work on another. Say you like the idea about the high-school prom and the girl you almost danced with.

What can be done with this? Let's say the hero of this story is a brainy but shy young man who has fallen in love with a girl, without ever once speaking to her. The love is unrequited—that's his dilemma. His name is Otto; her name is Sheila. He knows only that she's new in town and that her father is a millionaire. Seeing her, he's paralyzed with fear. He can't approach her. Do we have a premise? Not yet. It might be "great love leads to—?," but we don't know for sure.

So you let your imagination run, and here's what you come up with: During the summer following high school, Otto passes by Sheila's house and sees her sunbathing, swimming in her pool, and the like. His throat closes up. His glasses steam. He tries to walk up close to the fence to talk to her, but his knees go weak. He finally gets up the courage to phone her. Yes, she remembers seeing him around, she says. And yes, she'll go out with him. They begin dating. He is so in love with her that when he's near her he stutters. She's interested in him at first, because of what a brain he's supposed to be, but she soon becomes bored with him. He just isn't fun, and Sheila is a fun girl. So she starts making excuses why she can't go out with him. He falls into despair. He becomes morose, perhaps suicidal.

If he kills himself, your premise would be: "great love leads to suicide."

If he finds happiness with another, more sincere, girl: "unrequited love leads to acceptance of another's love."

If he buries himself in work: "unrequited love leads to workaholism."

THE THREE C'S OF PREMISE

There is no formula for constructing premises, but according to Egri, every good premise should contain an element of *character* which through *conflict* leads to a *conclusion*. A coward goes to war and becomes a hero. A brave man goes into battle and becomes a coward. Samson has his hair cut and loses his great powers, but he gets them back. When you formulate your premise, remember the three C's: character, conflict, and conclusion. A dramatic story is the transformation of character through crisis; the premise is a succinct statement of that transformation.

Is it okay, you may wonder, to use a premise that has been used before? Absolutely. Premises are free for the taking. Flaubert's *Madame Bovary* and Tolstoy's *Anna Karenina* have the same premise (illicit love leads to death). So do scores of lesser novels that have made it in the market place. How many novels could be written on the Samson and Delilah theme? Dozens and dozens. Ever read a story in which a plain but deserving girl finally marries Mr. Wonderful? It has been done a trillion times and will be done a trillion times more. So steal all the premises you want. Every novelist in America could write a novel, say, with the premise "greed leads to fulfillment" and no two would be proved the same way.

PREMISE AND SELECTIVITY

Selectivity—choosing what to include and what to omit in a novel—is an important part of the writer's work. A writer is exercising good selectivity when he leaves out scenes, descriptions, characters, and dialogue that the story can do without. When a writer exercises good selectivity, the reader perceives the story as being "tight." When the writer exercises poor selectivity, the reader perceives the story as being "bloated." Knowing your premise will allow you to know the difference. To illustrate how a writer might use a premise to assist in selectivity, let's take a look first at how it might be done in a nonfiction book. Say you had it in mind to write a book on Harry S. Truman. You want to call it *The Times of Truman*. You're thinking of including the following topics:

1. An account of Harry Truman's courtship of his wife, Bess.
2. An account of Harry Truman's career as a haberdasher.
3. A collection of Bess Truman's favorite recipes.
4. A critique of the Truman Doctrine.
5. Harry Truman's retirement years in retrospect.

Now then, which of these would you select to be included in your nonfiction book? You can't tell, because a book entitled *The Times of Truman* could include any of these topics or none of them. What does your choice depend on? It depends on your premise, on what you are trying to say, or to prove. If you intend to write a personal history, Bess's favorite recipes might be worth including; if you're writing a political analysis, they would not. A critique of the Truman Doctrine should be included if you are writing about his political career, but not if you are writing about his personal life. Selectivity—what goes in and what doesn't—is determined by your premise.

In a work of fiction the author's exercise of selectivity is similarly determined by the premise. Say you want to write a story which proves the premise, "love leads to loneliness."

Your protagonist is Henry Percible. He operates a lighthouse, alone, on a rock on the Farallon Islands, out in the Pacific Ocean twenty miles from San Francisco. He loves peace and quiet, feeding his goldfish, and going for walks to the end of his island.

He takes a two-week leave to tour Northern California and see some redwoods. He meets Julie, your heroine, and they fall passionately in love. After a whirlwind courtship, they marry and go to live on Henry's island.

Henry had always considered himself a contented man; now he considers himself a blissful one. Julie loves the island; she plants some flowers, fixes up their little cottage, takes walks with Henry in the afternoon, helps him polish the lens on the lighthouse searchlight.

Then Henry receives distressing news. His aged mother is critically ill. He flies to Florida to be at her bedside, leaving Julie in charge of the lighthouse. His mother dies and Henry stays on a few days to handle the arrangements, then returns to his island, where, after a couple of weeks,

Henry is over his grief and he and Julie resume their happy lives together.

November comes, and the fog rolls in and the sea turns nasty. It rains every day. Julie grows irritable. She begins to hate the island. Her garden is destroyed by hail. The cottage is too cold for her; she longs to go where it's warm and sunny. She begs and pleads with Henry; finally he consents. They move to Arizona.

There, Henry gets a job driving a bus, which he hates. He finds Arizona too dry, too hot, too sunny, and even though they live in a small town, he feels hemmed in by people. He longs to return to his solitary Farallons. He calls his old boss and finds he can have his old job back.

Now it's Henry who begs and pleads. He can't stand being away from the quiet hum of the old lighthouse, the smell of the sea, the crashing of the waves. Won't she give it another try? He'll insulate the cottage, get her a VCR, a cat to keep her company, etc.

Seeing how totally miserable he is, she agrees to go back to the island.

Once there, however, it doesn't take her long to realize she will never be able to last. She hates it more than ever, and one night she steals away on the launch, leaving a note behind telling him not to try to find her.

Henry doesn't try. He knows he could never leave the island and she could never learn to love it as he does.

He stays on the island, but what was once welcome solitude is now crushing loneliness. The premise has been proved: "love leads to loneliness."

Say you're satisfied that your story does prove the premise. But proving the premise isn't enough. It must be proved *economically.* Aristotle put it this way:

> The story, as an imitator of action, must represent one action, a complete whole, with its several incidents so closely connected that the transposal or withdrawal of any one of them will disjoin and dislocate the whole. For that which makes no perceptible difference by its presence or absence is no real part of the whole.

In other words, if a part of the story does not help to prove the premise, that part should be cut out. In the story above, the trip Henry makes to Florida makes no difference to the further complications and developments of the story. The premise "love leads to loneliness" is proved completely without Henry having taken that trip. The scenes that take place between Henry and his dying mother may be the greatest scenes in the story, full of trauma and pathos, but if they do not contribute to proving the premise, they must go. No ifs, ands, or buts about it.

The premise, Egri says, is a *tyrant.* Once the author formulates his premise, every scene, every line of dialogue, every narrative description, every sentence, every word should contribute to the proving of that premise. Are there no exceptions? you ask. The rules of writing dramatic fiction are not rules at all, but principles. Any principle may be violated if the writer can get away with it. Melville got away with it in *Moby-Dick,* which featured lengthy asides on whaling and is greatly admired for it. If you attempt it, however, you do so at your peril. For every writer who attempts it and succeeds, there are a thousand who don't.

What is the premise of this chapter? "Every dramatic story has one and only one premise."

THE UNCONSCIOUS WRITER

Shocking as it may seem, some theorists don't believe in the concept of premise. One of them is Kenneth MacGowan who, in *A Primer of Playwriting* (1951), explains Egri's theory of premise in some detail, but then says, "I suppose it [finding your premise] is merely a harmless little exercise in the manufacture of bromides . . . all it amounts to is saying a good play will have a moral message." MacGowan has come to this conclusion because of the many writers who sell fiction by the truckload but have never heard of premise. They write by instinct, and some of them have very good instincts indeed.

Jean Z. Owen tells about her days as an instinctual writer in *Professional Fiction Writing* (1974). She says that when she was an aspiring writer, she would, like most aspiring writers, "listen respectfully whenever anyone discussed characterization or dialogue or viewpoint, and was likely to genuflect mentally at the mere mention of plotting," but when it came to premise (which she calls "theme"), she "brushed aside the subject as being inconsequential."

One day she was discussing a proposed novel with an editor. She says she had her notes in order, a solid story idea, "an impressive dossier" on the major characters, and an over-elaborate outline.

Then the editor asked her about her premise.

Puzzled, she said she hadn't really thought about it.

Then the editor said they didn't have anything to discuss.

Stunned, Ms. Owen says she went home and thought long

and hard about it. She reviewed every story she had ever written in terms of premise and came to an amazing conclusion: *most of the stories she had not sold did not have a premise, and every one she had sold did have a premise!*

"Since that time," she says, "I have cashed a great many checks for stories, novelettes, and novels that would never have sold without the knowledge I culled from the episode."

So how did Ms. Owen write stories with a strong premise without knowing it? Simple. She is a talented writer with a strong story sense. She was working intuitively. She had characters in conflict and usually things would come to a conclusion that felt right. And it turned out that it was right.

The resistance to the idea of having a premise, as Ms. Owen says, is often formidable. Aspiring writers often ask, "If you can write a great story without knowing your premise, why bother trying to figure it out?" Some even believe it is not only a bother, but potentially destructive as well. One such person once told me: "Look, what if a writer *can* tell a terrific story with living characters who grow through conflict—along with all the other elements of a good novel—without using the notion of premise? I submit to you (said in a high moral tone) that your preaching about having to have a premise could be terribly dangerous to him because he may feel that he has done something terribly wrong if his book has no easily identifiable premise—and therefore go on to impose something destructive on an otherwise fine story!"

The answer to such a charge is this: If the characters develop through conflict leading to a conclusion, then the book has a good premise; it's inescapable, even if the writer is unconscious of what it is.

Knowing your premise will simply insure that your instincts are correct. A premise is no more, Egri says, than a shorthand way of saying, "Character through conflict leads to a conclusion."

No dramatic story has ever been written that is anything other than *character through conflict leading to a conclusion.*

Character, conflict, and premise are the bricks, the mortar, and the form of a story. What comes next is the blueprint, the stepsheet, which makes storytelling as easy as ABC.

4.

THE ABC'S OF STORYTELLING

WHAT'S A STORY?

A STORY is a "narrative of events."

Little Red Riding Hood goes into the woods, meets the wolf, takes a short cut to grandma's, meets the wolf again, says "My, what big teeth you have," and the woodcutter comes and chops up the wolf. A narrative of events is a simple recounting or retelling of something that happened, either in the "real" world, or in a "fictional" world. The story of Little Red Riding Hood is clearly a narrative of events. It is also a narrative of events when the old man goes out to catch the big fish, or when Michael Corleone goes out to kill his father's enemies, or when Leamas, the spy, goes out into the cold. Any story is a narrative of events. But that is not all it is.

Consider this narrative of events:

Joe hops out of bed, dresses, packs a lunch, gets into his car. He drives a few blocks to his girlfriend's place and picks her up. Her name is Sally. They drive to the beach where they lie on the hot sand all day, then have a nice seafood dinner. On the way home they stop for ice cream. This is a narrative of events, but is it a story?

Most readers, instinctively, would sense that it is not.

The reason is that the events are not worth reading about. The events must be of interest. So what if Joe goes to the beach with his girlfriend? So what if they have a dinner? The events of this narrative have no meaning because the events have no consequences. If we define a story as a "narrative of events," we have not gone far enough in our definition. We must add that it is a "narrative of *consequential* events."

But is that all there is to it?

What if I told you the sufferings and travails of a rubber tree being pruned? Or the trials and tribulations of a motorboat as it makes its way up the Congo. Not interested? It would only be interesting if the rubber tree or the motorboat had human characteristics. Jonathan Livingston Seagull was a humanlike seagull. Jonathan Livingston Seagull and the little locomotive who said, "I think I can" are interesting characters not because they are a bird and a train, but because they are humans in odd shapes.

So a story involves not only consequential events, but consequential events *involving human characters.* And not only human characters, but human characters that are worthy of our attention. No one wants to read about characters who are just anybody. They want to read about interesting somebodies, characters capable of evoking in the reader some measure of emotional response.

An expanded definition of story now would be: "A story is a narrative of events involving worthy human characters and consequential events."

This definition is good but still not complete. What is missing is that the characters *must change* as a result of conflict. If a character waltzes through a story unaffected by the events and sufferings he sees and endures, then the narrative of events is not a story at all, but merely an adventure. A complete definition, then, is:

   A story is a narrative of consequential events involving worthy human characters who change as a result of those events.

THE DRAMATIC STORY

In a dramatic story, the only kind generally worth reading, the characters will struggle. You may write a story in which the characters suffer and are involved in events, but are generally passive, doing nothing to solve their problems. If the characters change as a result of the hardships inflicted on them, such a narrative of events will be a story, but it will not be a dramatic story. Characters must struggle if you are to have drama. A reader may sympathize with the plight of a suffering character, but true reader identification—where readers will forget themselves and be completely absorbed into the character's world—can only happen with a character who is struggling. Remember Joe and Sally? Let's present them a dilemma to struggle with and see what happens:

> When Joe left the house that morning for Sally's, he noticed a beat-up van following him. Why would anyone be following him? he wondered. Must be his imagination, he told himself.

Interested? Of course. Something mysterious is occurring. We want to know what will happen. We might have also started the story this way:

> Joe bought the half-carat ring at a discount jewelry store down by the waterfront. That night at the restaurant he was going to "pop the question." Sure he had only known her two weeks, but for him two weeks was plenty of time . . .

Are we interested? Of course. We want to know if she'll say yes and how it will affect him when she does. How about a spooky story?

> Joe hadn't thought about it for months, but when he was getting his swim trunks out of his drawer, what the gypsy had said at the Christmas party the year before came back to him: "You are destined for a watery grave soon, my son . . ."

The dilemmas you present to your characters are called "story questions." Story questions make the reader want to read on to find the answers. They are the appetizers of the feast you are serving up.

BEGINNING THE STORY
BEFORE THE BEGINNING

Where, then, do you start your narrative of consequential events involving worthy human characters?

Usually, you begin just before the beginning.

This is not as contradictory as it sounds. If you look at a man's life in its entirety, there will be high spots and low spots, good times and bad. You will select from that life one particular story to tell, say the time your subject got fired from Bromberg & Bromberg and went into business for himself. You choose this story to tell because it is, in your opinion, potentially the most dramatic, exciting, and fresh.

Where exactly would you begin to relate your narrative of events? The best place would probably be just before the firing. The firing itself marks the beginning of the story. But we can't understand the impact of the firing unless we understand what the character's situation was before he was fired. Is the firing a good thing or a bad thing for him? If it's a horrible job and the character should leave it, the firing is a relief. If he needs the job desperately and the firing represents impending ruin, you have a totally different situation. Events can only be understood within the context of the character's situation at the time the event occurs; therefore it's important to the reader to know the *status quo situation*, which is the state of things at a particular time.

The events prior to the firing take place within the status quo situation. The core conflict (his struggle to get started in his own business) would begin at the firing.

- Michael Corleone in *The Godfather* is a war hero; he considers himself patriotic and law-abiding, and in the opening of *The Godfather* he is contemptuous of his father's illegal business. This is the status quo situation before the pivotal character (the character who forces the action), Sollozzo, attempts to get the Corleone family involved in the drug business. Sollozzo's offer is the event that begins the core conflict of *The Godfather*.
- In *One Flew over the Cuckoo's Nest*, the narrative begins before McMurphy enters the ward

(the status quo situation). The story begins with McMurphy's arrival a few pages later.

- At the beginning of A *Christmas Carol*, before the arrival of the ghosts, Scrooge has conflicts with his clerk, his nephew, and two gentlemen who come seeking a charitable gift. These conflicts occur within the status quo situation. The core conflict begins later with the arrival of the ghosts.

- *The Spy Who Came in from the Cold* begins at the end of Leamas's previous assignment (the status quo situation). We see him as the cool professional at the top of his form before he gets his new assignment—to go behind the Iron Curtain posing as a defector.

- Hemingway started *The Old Man and the Sea* the evening before the old man goes out to catch the big fish (the status quo situation). When he rows out to sea the next day to try to catch the fish the core conflict begins.

- Flaubert opens *Madame Bovary* with Charles Bovary married to his first wife (the status quo situation), long before we meet Emma, the protagonist of the novel.

- In *Lolita*, Nabokov gives us Humbert Humbert's biography (the status quo situation) well before he shows us Lolita. We understand completely his need for her, even before we meet her.

Just as the playwright sets the stage, as the opera has an overture, as the Constitution has a preamble, the fiction writer depicts the status quo situation. It shows the reader the fictive world as it is before the events of the core conflict begin to unfold. It is the soup and salad before the entree.

THE ALTERNATIVES

If you choose not to begin before the beginning, not to depict the status quo situation, you are faced with the problem of simultaneously introducing the character and the dilemma he's facing, then filling the reader in on the character's status quo situation later. Say you choose to begin your story at the exact moment of the beginning, the moment of the firing:

> Joe held the pink slip in his hand, feeling an icy chill run up his spine. He looked across the desk at the boss, who was staring back impassively, the smoldering stub of a cigar jammed in his mouth.

Since we don't know Joe or his situation, we don't know whether his being fired is justifed. The reader therefore withholds sympathy for Joe until he finds out. Forcing your reader to withhold sympathy at the opening of your story is not a wise move on the part of the writer. At the beginning you want to gain sympathy for your protagonist as quickly as possible.

Another alternative is to begin *after* the beginning of the story:

> Joe walked down Fifth Avenue in a misting rain carrying a box full of junk he'd just cleaned out of his desk. How can I tell Sara that I've been fired, he thought, when we've just bought the new Porsche?

The problem here is that not only do we miss knowing Joe before the firing, but we miss what is potentially a very dramatic scene: the firing itself. That scene could, of course, be retold in a flashback, but since we would then already know the outcome of the firing scene, and would already have seen the impact the firing had on the character, much of the scene's tension and suspense would be lost.

Better to start before the beginning. The reader will know the character and will sympathize with him, and you can dramatize the change in the status quo situation that marks the beginning of the story.

INCIDENT AND CHARACTER: HOW EACH GROWS OUT OF THE OTHER

Aristotle said in *The Poetics* that the length of a drama should be such that the hero passes "by a series of probable or necessary stages from misfortune to happiness, or from happiness to misfortune." Twenty-three centuries later, Egri says the same thing when he insists that a character should "grow from pole to pole." A coward becomes brave, a lover becomes an enemy, a saint becomes a sinner—this is growth from pole to pole.

When you plan your novel you will need to plan not only the incidents, but the stages of the characters' development (or as Egri and others call it, "growth") as well. In order to have a rising conflict, the character must be developing, changing through stages, growing incrementally from pole to pole. This can be done at the planning stage of the novel through the use of a stepsheet.

A stepsheet is a detailed plan of the incidents of a story. Using a stepsheet is the way an author keeps control of his story. Think of it as a blueprint. You are strongly urged to make one. Here is what a stepsheet describing the "steps" (incidents) of a story might look like:

A.   Scrooge, a "squeezing, wrenching, grasping,
scraping, clutching, covetous old sinner! Hard
and sharp as flint" (in the words of Dickens), is
a businessman in London. It's the nineteenth
century. Life is bleak. Scrooge is friendless and
alone, and likes it that way. His business partner,
Marley, has been dead for seven years. It's Christmas Eve and Scrooge is visited by his nephew,
who has come to wish him a merry Christmas.
Scrooge, angered by the interruption of his work,
dismisses him with a "Bah, humbug!"

B.   Two gentlemen come to collect money for
the poor. Scrooge asks them if the workhouses
are still in use. When they answer that they are,
Scrooge says good and throws them out. Now
Scrooge has "an improved opinion of himself,"
says Dickens, and is in a more "facetious temper
than was usual with him."

C.   Scrooge then tells his clerk, Bob Cratchit,
that he can have Christmas off if he will be in
"all the earlier the next morning." Scrooge walks
off with a growl and takes a "melancholy" dinner
in his usual "melancholy" tavern, then goes home
to his "gloomy suite of rooms."

These first three events have occurred within the status quo
situation. They merely set the stage; the core conflict between
Scrooge and the ghosts has not yet begun. This is a portrait of
Scrooge as he was in his daily life perhaps for years. In other
words, the reader is given an understanding of the status quo
situation, and then the core conflict begins:

D.   The first weird event happens: As he gets
home, Scrooge sees Marley's face projected on

the front door knocker. He dismisses it as a hal-
lucination and goes up to his rooms. "Humbug!"
he says. The story has begun.

E.   Now the ghost of Marley appears with a great
clanking of chains. "It's humbug still," says
Scrooge. "I won't believe it!" But the ghost speaks,
and finally Scrooge does believe it. The ghost
tells him he will be visited by three spirits. "I—
I think I'd rather not," says Scrooge.

The events of the story so far have changed him. He has
"grown" from being able to dismiss the apparition as "humbug"
to being afraid. "Couldn't I just take'em all at once and have it
over with, Jacob?" he asks the ghost. Scrooge has been humbled.

F.   Marley's ghost leaves. After it has gone,
Scrooge tries to say "humbug" but can't (growth).
He goes to bed and falls into a deep sleep. End
of chapter 1. (Chapter 2 begins with the arrival
of the first of the three spirits, the Ghost of Christmas Past.)

As you can see, the stepsheet reflects the events of the story
in a shorthand way, and gives an indication of how the characters
grow, allowing the author to keep his story in control. Earlier
we discussed a new novel involving Boyer Bennington Mitchell,
private eye. Here is how a stepsheet of that novel might look:

A.   Boyer Bennington Mitchell is in his office.
Things haven't been going well since he took
over the private eye business from his father, Big
Jake. Most of Big Jake's clients, accustomed to
his tough methods, have left. The few who have
remained are sleazy lawyers who don't pay their

bills and out-of-town detectives who can't pay
theirs. Boyer's secretary comes in to quit because
Boyer has paid her with an IOU. After she leaves,
he paces and worries. He has no cases to work
on. A man shows up, pretending to be a client,
but he's a process server. Boyer is being sued for
his back rent on his office.

B.   Despondent, Boyer goes home. He's single
and lives with his mother. His mother tries to
get him to give up this "stupid business." She
has a friend who owns a stock brokerage and will
give him a job. But he doesn't want to be a
stockbroker, he wants to be a detective, and he
tells his mother so very firmly. Standing up to
her has given Boyer new vigor. (Everything to
this point is within the status quo situation). Seeing
his determination, his mother acquiesces and tells
him that an acquaintance was asking if the family
was still in the business. Hoping he would quit,
she hadn't wanted to give him a referral, but since
she sees now there's no way he'll ever quit, she
gives him the woman's name. This marks the
beginning of the core conflict of the story.

C.   The woman, Lydia Wickham, is soon to be
a murderer. Part of her plan is to hire Boyer
ostensibly to find out who "the other woman" is
in her husband's life (neither Boyer nor the reader
knows of her plan, of course). She gives Boyer
two thousand dollars as a retainer, and he leaves
in a state of buoyant optimism (more growth).

D.   Boyer spends the next five days "shadowing"
her husband and finds no evidence that he is
seeing any other woman. Boyer gets weary and

thinks he may be taking Lydia Wickham's money
for nothing.

E.   Boyer reports back to Lydia; she tells him to
keep following her husband. He reluctantly agrees
because he needs the money.

F.   That night he witnesses, for the first time,
the husband skulking around . . .

In a well-constructed story, the events (A, B, C, D, E, etc.)
are *causal*. Event B cannot happen unless event A happens. Event
C cannot happen unless events A and B happen. Readers have
a powerful desire to read what will happen next because they
expect the events they have witnessed to have repercussions. The
cause-and-effect nature of the events makes for a finely woven
tapestry. When readers say a story is "tight" or critics say a story
is "not tight enough" they are referring to this cause-and-effect
relationship.

The events of a story, the conflicts, have an effect on the
characters, so that the way in which they respond to conflict
changes as the story moves along. Let's examine another stepsheet
and take a close look at the changes in the main character as he
progresses through the story:

A.   Andy Simms, nineteen, is a Caspar Milquetoast. It's 1968 and the Vietnam War is going
full fury. He worries about being drafted. He
studies like mad to maintain a C average in college so he can keep his student deferment. His
major is sociology because it's easy for him to get
good grades in it. This is the status quo situation
at the beginning of the novel. The stage is set.

B.   Andy's girlfriend, Hilda, wants him to be an
engineer. How can he make anything of himself

in sociology? Engineering is where the bucks are, she says. At first Andy resists, but, fearing he will lose her, he gives in. He changes his major to engineering. This is the beginning of the story.

C.   Engineering is extremely difficult for Andy. He gives it all he's got, but the best he can do is to get D grades. He starts drinking. Drinking makes it harder for him to study. He becomes more and more anxious. At the end of the semester he gets poor grades and loses his student deferment. Once classified 1-A, he falls into despondency. He mopes constantly. He becomes irritable and short-tempered and his friends desert him.

D.   Hilda drops Andy because she considers him a loser. Andy's despondency becomes a full-blown psychotic depression; now he can't even get out of bed in the morning.

E.   He is drafted into the army. When he reports for duty he is having a schizophrenic episode. He goes through the induction process hardly knowing where he is. The idea of running away to Canada occurs to him, but he doesn't seriously consider it. It would make him feel like a traitor. He loves his country; it's the military he hates. At this point in the story, Andy is at the nadir of his character development. He is anxiety-ridden, lonely, and afraid; he feels incompetent and dejected.

F.   In boot camp, Andy soon finds that if he doesn't complain and just does as he's told, the sergeants won't be too hard on him. He also finds that he has a good shooting eye and is a marksman with an M-16 rifle. For the first time in his life, he has found something he is naturally good at. His platoon wins the camp shooting contest with Andy as the lead shooter. Andy has the best score in the whole camp. In addition, though he isn't physically strong, he has much more endurance than he ever imagined; he is always first to finish the twenty-mile forced marches. Andy is finding self-respect through his struggles and triumphs in the army. He's developing, finding his strength.

G.   Disaster strikes. Andy is picked to go to Vietnam. He had hoped to get into clerk's school, but his success in boot camp has sealed his fate. They need sharpshooters. Off he goes to Vietnam, full of fear and trepidation. Only his newfound pride in what he accomplished at boot camp sustains him—Andy's character development is tested and proved.

H.   Andy is assigned to a jungle reconnaissance patrol. He's terrified and sullen, hardly able to eat, a regression to his former state of high anxiety, but he's not giving in to it as he once might have. He finds the strength to endure. It is on the reconnaissance patrol that his sharpshooting prowess serves him well. His unit is pinned down for four hours by murderous machine-gun fire. They figure they have one chance, and that is to rush the enemy. It's suicidal, but if they can knock out the machine gun, at least some of them may survive.

I.   Andy thinks this is crazy. He disobeys orders and sneaks off into the jungle, climbs a cliff, and when dawn comes, he's in position to fire down on the machine gunners and drive them off. His

buddies are able to escape when the enemy gives
their full attention to knocking out Andy. It proves
too much for them, though. Andy can pick them
off as they start up the cliff. They figure it isn't
worth it to get one man, and withdraw. Andy is
a hero. Subsequently, he is awarded the Silver
Star. In terms of his development, Andy is now
at an extremely high point. He's proud, optimistic, full of confidence in himself and his future.

J.   When he comes home, Hilda wants to make
up with him. But Andy is no longer a milquetoast, and he won't be bullied by her. Instead,
he moves to California, where he intends to go
back to college and become a sociologist. He's
his own man now, having conquered his terror.
He has grown from one pole (terrified, intensely
pessimistic) to the opposite pole (self-confident,
optimistic).

THE USES OF THE STEPSHEET

There are no formal rules for making up a stepsheet. Some writers
put in a great amount of detail; others make theirs sketchy and
thin. It is up to the author. The purpose of the stepsheet is to
keep events in a progressive cause-and-effect order, A-B-C-D-E-
F, and so on, and to chart the growth and development of the
characters.

Can you decide to change the stepsheet later on—for instance,
when you are three-quarters through the first draft? What if you
get to the scene where the patrol is pinned down and you think
it would be better if Andy got wounded? Okay, fine. But being
wounded has an effect on the rest of the story. You will have to

modify the subsequent steps. What effect does being wounded have on his getting the Silver Star? If he's disfigured or crippled, what will that do to his confidence and newfound pride? Before making any changes, think through the consequences. Then if you decide it would make a better story, go right ahead and make the change. The stepsheet is a guide, not a straitjacket.

Complications, the events or steps of your story, do not spring to life by themselves. They are brought to life by the inertia of the events that preceded them in time. This is the *logic* of story writing, and it is this logic that gives your story its organic unity.

5.

RISING TO THE CLIMAX, OR, THE PROOF OF THE PUDDING IS IN THE PREMISE

CLIMAX, RESOLUTION, AND YOU

- Think of a climax as the target and the rest of your story as the flight of the arrow.
- Think of a climax as the other shore toward which you are building the bridge of your book.
- Think of a climax as the goal line where the winning touchdown is made.
- Think of a climax as the knockout punch of the heavyweight prizefight of your novel.

Or think of it like this:

- A story is a question mark; a climax, an exclamation!
- A story is tension; a climax, satisfaction.
- A story is the face-off, the quick draw, the pull of the trigger; the climax is the bullet between the eyes.
- The climax is the last, for which the first was made.

The tension of a story rises through its complications to a point at which the core conflict is settled. The characters have been tested, they have been pushed and punished; as a result, they have gone through stages of development. As the tension rises to the climax things are coming to a head. The pressures on the characters build to the "breaking point"; the climax is that point. The core conflict must now be settled. How then do you settle it?

It is settled in what Egri calls a *revolution*.

The Greeks had a name for this revolution. They called it *Peripety*. Aristotle explains it this way in *The Poetics*:

A Peripety is the change from one state of things within the play to its opposite, and that too is the probable or necessary sequence of events . . . this, with a Discovery will arouse either pity or fear —actions of that nature being what Tragedy is assumed to represent; and it will also serve to bring about the happy or unhappy ending.

In *The Basic Patterns of Plot* (1959), William Foster-Harris says it this way:

Here is what [fiction] writing is trying to tell: *the answer to any possible problem or question you could pose is always in some fantastic manner the diametric reversal of the question.* (Emphasis in the original.)

In the climax, the coward finds his courage, the reluctant lover agrees to marry, the losers win, the winners lose, the saints commit sin, the sinners are redeemed. This is what is meant by "revolution." It is a reversal: things are somehow turned upside down.

- In *A Christmas Carol*, the climax comes when the Ghost of Christmas Yet to Come shows Scrooge his own empty death and Scrooge, in terror, pleads to be allowed to change. When Scrooge wakes up, he finds it's Christmas morning. He has been sojourning with ghosts and now he's back among people. He has been shown his death, and now he's alive once again. There is indeed a revolution at the climax.
- In *The Godfather*, it appears that the Corleone family has been reduced to nothing, that they are leaving New York, beaten and in disgrace. Then Michael Corleone strikes with awesome fury against his enemies, getting his full revenge in a single day of destruction. The family's reputation and position are restored. This is certainly revolutionary.
- Leamas, in *The Spy Who Came in from the Cold*, is apparently home free at the point of the climax. All he has to do is climb over the fence and he will be out of East Germany, but betrayal by his superiors has destroyed his will to live; he chooses death instead. Another revolutionary turnaround.

- It looks as if Big Nurse has won when she has McMurphy lobotomized. She has been winning victory after victory throughout *One Flew over the Cuckoo's Nest*. But Kesey is proving that the human spirit is uncrushable. The other patients find their courage, and one—the Chief—finds his soul and smashes his way out of the cuckoo's nest. So at the climax there is a quite satisfying revolution.

- Lolita leaves Humbert Humbert in the climax of *Lolita*. Even though her departure is heavily foreshadowed, it is still a revolutionary development in the story. What follows is Humbert Humbert's rapid descent into insanity, in which the man of love becomes the man of hate.

- The old man in *The Old Man and the Sea* is apparently washed up at the beginning of the novel because he has not caught a fish in eighty-four days. He's a laughingstock. When he lands the great fish, everything changes. Still another revolution.

- Emma's climactic suicide in *Madame Bovary* is certainly revolutionary. The woman who wanted to "live it up" embraces death.

Story is *struggle*. You begin your narrative just before the protagonist is presented with a dilemma, at the point of attack. The character struggles with the dilemma; the dilemma worsens into a crisis. The crisis rises to a point where it must be resolved. An action is taken, bringing about the climax. The result is either favorable or unfavorable, but the crisis is over. In either case the entire situation changes; there is a revolution no matter which way it goes.

CLIMAX, PREMISE, RESOLUTION,
AND HOW NOT TO GET IT
ALL CONFUSED

The ending of a story is often described in terms of "climax" and "resolution" as if they were two separate entities. But the boundaries of the climax and those of the resolution are impossible to determine in most cases. The climax might be thought of as a point, a moment, the precise instant the reader perceives that the core conflict is settled. That precise moment might be when Godzilla is killed, when the heroine says yes to the marriage proposal, when the winning point is scored, when the battle is won, when the condemned man dies. Although the climactic moment is the point at which the core conflict is settled, it does not prove the premise. The premise is proved by the climax-resolution as an entity.

Let's say you've decided to write a story and want to prove the premise "ruthless ambition brings glory and fame." This premise, as Egri says all good premises should do, suggests three things: character, conflict, and conclusion. The ruthless ambition is, of course, a trait of one of the characters, the protagonist. You decide on a name, "Martin Crenshaw." If he is going to achieve wealth and fame, Martin Crenshaw must have an arena in which he can seek them. Say it's politics. Martin is going to run for senator. Now, if he is ruthless, he will do whatever he has to do to become a senator. Will he lie? Sure. Will he cheat? You bet he will. Will he murder? Well, maybe he'll stop short of that.

The target of your novel, the climax, will come when the issue of Martin's becoming a senator is settled. Since your premise is that ruthless ambition leads to glory and fame, you know from the start he is going to make it. Along the way he will stuff ballot boxes, buy off special interests, smear his primary opponents, spy on editorial writers, and so on. His family relationships will be strained to the breaking point. His mother may disown him.

Pressures will mount as election day draws near. Now comes election night and we're counting the ballots. Martin wins! In the resolution we see him basking in his fame with wealth just around the corner, reconciling with his family and opponents, and pledging to be the best senator the state has ever seen. Your premise is proved by the climax (the moment he wins) and the resolution which follows (the reconciliations).

Don't like that story? You say you'd prefer that ruthless ambition lead to something else? Disaster? Death? Degradation? Okay. Let's see how that would work. Our new premise would be (like Macbeth) "ruthless ambition leads to death."

Martin is ruthless. He wants to be a senator. He lies. cheats, bribes, and so on. His wife leaves him. His mother disowns him. His children become communists. He is not swayed from his goal. Nothing can stop Martin. On the night before the election his pollster shows that the race is a dead heat. He can't stand the idea that he might lose. He is driven to the brink of insanity, gets a gun, and takes a shot at his opponent from ambush the morning of the election. A pen in the opponent's pocket deflects the bullet and he is only scratched. The publicity over the miraculous event excites the voters, who elect Martin's opponent in a landslide. Martin falls into despondency, gets drunk, and mumbles something to the wrong person about being the guy who shot at his opponent. He is exposed as the attempted assassin and, facing disgrace and prison, kills himself. The target we have been shooting for, the climactic moment, is in this case not the election but the suicide. This is where the ruthless ambition has led.

THE PATTERN OF
RESOLVING CONFLICT

Conflict that comes after the climax, after the core conflict is settled, is "resolving conflict."

In a story, the conflicts grow and intensify, the stakes rise, and the situation becomes more desperate up to the climactic moment. This is rising conflict. Then—pow!—the climax. Now, the conflicts that follow have the opposite pattern. The storm is receding; the intensity is lessening rather than increasing.

An event is "anticlimactic" if it has a rising conflict and comes after the core conflict is settled. No matter how inherently dramatic the event, the reader has little interest in it because the reader is now looking to see the effect of the climax on the characters.

Resolving conflict is often necessary to prove the premise and also to give the reader the feeling that the whole story has been told. Here's an example:

> He [Scrooge] had not gone far, when, coming on toward him he beheld the portly gentleman who had walked into his counting house the day before, and said, "Scrooge and Marley's, I believe?" It sent a pang across his heart to think how this old gentleman would look upon him when they met, but he knew what path lay straight before him, and he took it.
>
> "My dear sir," said Scrooge, quickening his pace, and taking the old gentleman by both his hands, "how do you do? I hope you succeeded yesterday. It was kind of you. A merry Christmas to you sir!"
>
> "Mr. Scrooge?"
>
> "Yes," said Scrooge. "That is my name, and I fear it may not be pleasant to you. Allow me to ask your pardon. And will you have the goodness—" Here Scrooge whispered in his ear.
>
> "Lord bless me!" cried the gentleman, as if his

breath were taken away. "My dear Mr. Scrooge,
are you serious?"

"If you please," said Scrooge. "Not a farthing
less. A great many back payments are included
in it, I assure you. Will you do me that favor?"

"My dear sir," said the other, shaking hands
with him, "I don't know what to say to such
munifi—"

"Don't say anything, please," retorted Scrooge.
"Come and see me. Will you come and see me?"

"I will!" cried the old gentleman . . .

You will notice there is no "insistence and resistance" as there
is in rising conflict. Think of resolving conflict as a winding down,
a settling of accounts, a mopping-up operation following the
decisive battle in a long war.

There are secondary conflicts which need resolving as well as
the core conflict. They may be resolved before or after the climax
of the core conflict.

The core conflict might be, say, Joe's struggle to get a job; a
strong secondary conflict might involve Joe and his wife, who
has left him during the course of the story. The outcome of the
conflict between Joe and his wife may not be settled at the climax,
where Joe accepts his new job; the question of Joe's reconciliation
with his wife would still need to be resolved. This could be done
by, say, having the break made permanent, or having the couple
happily reconcile, or you could suggest they *probably* will get
back together in the future. For example, she might agree to
have dinner with him. Something like that would indicate how
the conflict is likely to be resolved, which is often enough to
satisfy a reader. If all the strings are too neatly tied, the reader
may suspect the author of manipulation.

Some stories have no resolving conflict whatever, because all the questions are settled at the point of climax. The *Spy Who Came in from the Cold* climaxes and ends like this:

> They seemed to hesitate before firing again; someone shouted an order, and still no one fired. Finally they shot him, two or three shots. He stood glaring around him like a blinded bull in the arena. As he fell, Leamas saw a small car smashed between great lorries, and the children waving cheerfully through the window.

PROVING THE PREMISE OF THE CHARACTER

Each major character in a story has his own fate. Therefore, each character has a premise of his own. If you are proving in your story that "the big lie brings ruin," one character may be a liar; that does not mean all the characters must be liars. It simply means that *one* lie brings ruin.

Michael Corleone's ruling passion in *The Godfather* is love of his family. His love leads him to become the Don—the ruler of the family's illegal business—despite the fact that he is morally opposed to the business at the beginning of the story. His personal premise is "love of family leads to a life of crime." Michael has a brother, Sonny. Sonny also loves the family, but his personal premise is very different from Michael's. Sonny is animalistic. He is a hot-blooded warrior. When Sonny's sister is attacked by her husband, he rushes to her aid, even though he knows his enemies are looking for him and it might be a trap. He's gunned down. His premise: "hot-bloodedness leads to death."

In *One Flew over the Cuckoo's Nest* the climax comes when McMurphy is lobotomized. His premise is "challenging absolute authority leads to death." But there is more to the story. The Chief, because of the lessons taught him by McMurphy, is now able to regain his sanity and escape by smashing his way out. His premise is "acceptance (of McMurphy's code of manhood) leads to freedom." In his struggle to escape he is aided by the rest of the patients, proving that "the human spirit is uncrushable," which is the premise of the novel. Big Nurse, the tyrant, ends up with a rebellion on her hands. Her premise: "tyranny begets rebellion."

Madame Bovary's husband, Charles, loves his wife. She drives him to despair. "Love leads to despair" is his premise.

What is Bob Cratchit's premise? He sticks by Scrooge despite his vile ways. Things work out for him. His premise is "loyalty leads to happiness."

Characters are dynamic, not static. They are changeable. They develop: they find love where they had only loneliness; they build hope from hopelessness; they fall into disillusionment or despair from peaks of joy; and so on. Do not think of your characters as fixed. To have a vibrant, vigorous, gripping novel, *the characters must change as a result of conflict.* The character premise is a description of that change.

WHAT MAKES A GREAT CLIMAX?—THE SECRET OF SATISFYING A READER

The point of a joke is the punch line. The point of a novel is the climax-resolution. A joke, no matter how elaborate, how well told, how intriguing, is nothing without a great punch line. A dramatic novel, no matter how elaborate, how well told, how intriguing, is nothing without a good climax-resolution. To bring off a truly great climax-resolution, there are other elements to consider besides simply proving the premise.

First: Look for surprises.

As the reader nears the end of a book he senses that things are coming to a head. The reader knows there are not many pages left. The protagonist is into the sucking bog all the way up to his neck and it looks as if only a miracle can save him. The reader is certain he's doomed. Surprise: the protagonist uses his belt to reach a tree branch and gets himself out with a burst of strength and determination he didn't know he had.

The Corleone family is on the ropes; the old Godfather is dead; the family is being squeezed by the other Mafia families. Surprise: Michael Corleone, the new Don, savagely wipes out his enemies in a single day of retribution.

Scrooge is shown his gravestone. He's seen his own death. He appears finished. Surprise: he's not been shown what *will* happen, but only what *could* happen. He awakens and it's Christmas morning—he's saved!

When McMurphy is lobotomized it looks like the rebellion in the cuckoo's nest is over. Surprise: the Chief blasts his way out.

Leamas is home free. It's over. All he has to do is jump over the wall. Surprise: he chooses death.

Second: Exploit powerful emotions.

The reading of novels is primarily an emotional experience. In English 102A, The American Novel, 1800–1865, your professor taught you to hunt for hidden symbols and historical references, to look for vague literary allusions, to cull the philosophical nuances, to divine the sociological implications, to fathom the existential ramifications. This kind of nonsense has ruined a lot of writers as well as a lot of readers. The primary purpose in reading a novel is to experience at the emotional level the lives of the characters—to laugh with them, cry with them, suffer with them. Your primary object as a novelist is to move the reader emotionally.

A dramatic story builds to an apex of emotional concentration in the climax, at which point the skillful novelist will knock the reader over. When McMurphy is lobotomized the reader is shocked. When the old man catches the fish the reader stands up and cheers. When Leamas chooses death the reader is stunned. When Scrooge becomes giddy with delight at finding he hasn't missed Christmas, the reader becomes giddy right along with him. The reader pulls for Michael Corleone when he carries out his revenge. Who doesn't weep for Emma Bovary when she takes the poison, or for Humbert Humbert when he dies of despair?

Third: Issue a verdict in the Court of Poetic Justice.

What is justice? Justice is vindicating the innocent, punishing the guilty, and rewarding the virtuous. Poetic justice is punishment that fits the crime, or vindication that fits the virtue. To be "poetic," the agency dispensing the justice must be hidden. If the police do it, it isn't poetic. A man drowns his old spinster aunt in a bathtub. With the insurance money he buys a boat, which then sinks. He drowns. This is poetic justice because the agency (fate? accident? the Lord of the Universe?) that meted out the justice is not apparent, and the punishment (drowning) fits the crime (murder by drowning).

Suppose an ambitious man craves wealth, power, and glory. He dreams of the day when he and his wife can sit back on top of the heap and bask in their wealth. But his ambition hardens his heart and by the time he has made it to the top, crushing all his competitors, his wife has left him for a gentler, kinder man. He has achieved his goals, but the achievement is empty. That, too, is poetic justice.

If you can't give full vindication to the innocent or full rewards to the virtuous, let them at least have a slice of the pie. Readers crave to see justice done. Say you're writing a story of oppression. Your hero, a textile worker in a sweatshop, is trying to organize a union. The union is smashed; your hero has failed. In the court of poetic justice your villains have won. But if your hero has found courage, self-respect, and the love of a good woman, he has won something even more valuable—and there can be victories at other textile factories, other wars to fight and win. Even in death, a character can win something. Hamlet had his vengeance. McMurphy inspired the Chief.

Fourth: Find new facets of character.

If there are new aspects of character revealed at the climax, so much the better. Ah, so Joe Gocarefully finally found his guts, the reader says. Good for him! Your heroine finally wakes up to the fact that her lover is a cad. The good guys finally escape the prison camp. If the reader ends up cheering, you may have brought off a truly magnificent climax.

Fifth: The climax-resolution should make the novel whole.

In writing your novel you created story questions in the reader's mind. Some of these story questions, say, revolved around the main problem of the protagonist, an alcoholic. In the climax we find him joining Alcoholic Anonymous, or committing suicide. Either way, the core conflict is resolved. But there may be other, secondary questions that the reader is also worried about. Will the daughter continue to hate her father, will the wife be reconciled, will the ex-drunk get his job back? Only in melodrama, of course, will all these questions be answered fully, but even in a good drama, *some* of them should be answered fully and the rest should be answered at least in part. A good climax leaves the reader feeling that the story is finished.

- Scrooge has been transformed and will never be a miser again.
- The Corleones have regained their power.
- McMurphy is dead, but the Chief has found his soul and will never lose it.
- The old man has regained his respect.

6.

VIEWPOINT, POINT OF VIEW, FLASHBACKING, AND SOME NIFTY GADGETS IN THE NOVELIST'S BAG OF TRICKS

VIEWPOINT DEFINED

WHEN the author is describing a character and writes, "Marvin hated three things: stale donuts, his wife's meatloaf, and Republicans," he is revealing the character's *viewpoint*. A character's viewpoint is the combination of his collective opinions, prejudices, tastes, and attitudes. His viewpoint defines how the character interprets the world. The character's viewpoint grows out of his particular sociology, physiology, and psychology.

Viewpoint also refers to what might be called the *locus of narrative*. The locus of narrative refers to where the narrator stands in relation to the characters: as an unseen eyewitness acting as objective reporter; as a sort of divine know-it-all, able to read

- Leamas is dead.
- Humbert Humbert is dead.
- Emma Bovary is dead.

And this chapter is finished.

the thoughts and feelings of the characters; or as another character in the story.

OBJECTIVE VIEWPOINT

When the narrator is outside the characters at all times, writing as if he were a reporter, he is writing in *objective viewpoint*. The narrator describes the actions of the characters as if he were, say, watching a play. Here is an example:

> Joe awoke at three in the morning. He got up, went to the medicine chest, poured himself three fingers of something that fizzed, waited for it to stop bubbling, and drank it down holding his nose. Then he got dressed, loaded his shotgun, put it under his overcoat, jumped into his armored personnel carrier and drove to the bank . . .

This is called "objective" viewpoint because the narrator is *outside* the character, looking at the character "objectively," having no notion whatever about the "subjective" states of the characters. We are given nothing of what the character thinks and feels, what his attitudes are, what his plans are, and so on. It is written as if the narrator were a spectator simply copying down the dialogue and actions as he sees them happen.

Question: When do you use objective viewpoint? Answer: Very rarely.

Objective viewpoint is used when you want to create an air of mystery about a character. It's sometimes used in spy thrillers and detective novels when the villain is on stage. In a narrative written in objective viewpoint we see what the characters do without really knowing who they are. Readers will endure watching the skulking around of characters they don't really know in such cases because it is part of the fun.

Normally, readers are impatient with narratives in objective viewpoint because they want more intimacy with the characters and objective viewpoint offers the least intimacy. For this reason it is best to avoid it, and most writers do. There are, of course, notable exceptions. Dashiell Hammett's *The Maltese Falcon* is written in objective viewpoint, and is an acknowledged masterpiece. It is a difficult thing to pull off, however. Hammett went to great lengths in that novel to give the reader more intimacy with the characters through gestures, mannerisms, and facial expressions.

MODIFIED OBJECTIVE VIEWPOINT

One way to achieve more intimacy is through *modified objective viewpoint*. In modified objective viewpoint, the narrator does not claim to know the character's inner workings, but makes guesses about them. Sometimes the guesses prove wrong, resulting in what has been called an "unreliable narrator." In other words, in modified objective viewpoint the narrator describes honestly what is going on, what any sensible observer would see, and draws the same conclusions as the reader would. As long as the author does not cheat the reader, it's okay. But an unreliable narrator who is lying, or who is not telling all he should, is not an acceptable narrator to most readers.

Here's an example of modified objective viewpoint with an unreliable narrator who is not cheating:

> Phoebe awoke that morning snarling. She had had a fitful sleep. Maybe she was having bad dreams about Charlie. Maybe she'd caught a cold. Nobody really knows. It was found out later she

drove the old Chevy pickup into town that day and bought a used .38 Colt single-action and a box of shells for eighteen dollars. The clerk said she had a strange look in her eyes, full of hate. What thoughts must have gone through her head as she drove out to the old Tucker place. Images of her husband in bed with another woman flashed through her mind like lightning bolts, perhaps. She must have thought: I'm gonna kill that bitch! Then, as she came through the door in a cold, blind rage, she pointed the Colt at the two of them, pulling the trigger over and over again . . .

Even though the viewpoint is objective, the reader feels more intimacy with the character because the narrator has created the illusion of a subjective viewpoint. The narrator is not claiming he actually knows what goes on in the character's mind, but is only making assumptions. The viewpoint is objective because the narrator is viewing the character from the outside, giving no true report of subjective states.

The other common narrative viewpoints are all subjective, which means the narrator has access to the interior mental and emotional states of at least one character.

FIRST-PERSON SUBJECTIVE VIEWPOINT

The *first-person narrator* is always writing from a *subjective viewpoint*. The first-person narrator has access to one character, the narrator, who is himself a character in the story. He may be the protagonist, the antagonist, or any other character. In *Cuckoo's Nest* the story is narrated by the Chief, a minor character. *Lolita* is narrated by the protagonist, Humbert Humbert.

First-person narrative has many attractions, especially for the beginning novelist. A beginner often feels comfortable writing in first person; it is, after all, the way people write personal correspondence. And because a story narrated in the first person sounds like an eyewitness account, it has the added advantage of seeming more believable than a third-person account.

Most beginning writers choose a first-person narrator. And why not, you say, if it's more believable and the writer is more comfortable with it?

Here's why not: it takes considerable skill to handle a lengthy narrative from a single viewpoint. You cannot go places the narrator couldn't have been and show things to the reader the narrator couldn't have seen. Not without a lot of burdensome explaining.

Say you are using as first-person narrator the mother of the town "party girl." The narrator's daughter is seduced by the town Lothario when she's fourteen. It's an important scene and you want to show it. Since the mother was not there, how could she know what happened? Maybe the daughter tells her later. What if the daughter does not get along with her mother? How do you make it believable that the daughter would tell her mother anything?

A first-person narrator has the additional burden of showing how other characters feel strictly through how they look, speak, and act. This is a considerable challenge for an inexperienced writer.

It is also extremely difficult to write a lengthy narrative in the first person without boring the reader. The continuous use of "I" begins to sound, before long, like complaining when you are relating the character's feelings, and like bragging when you are relating the character's actions.

J. D. Salinger made it look easy in *The Catcher in the Rye.*

Raymond Chandler made it look easy with his Marlowe stories. J. D. Salinger and Raymond Chandler are responsible for many ruined first novels.

OMNISCIENT VIEWPOINT

If the narrator reveals what is going on in all the characters' heads, the story is in *omniscient viewpoint*. This is, of course, the most subjective of all possible viewpoints. Omniscient viewpoint was extremely popular in the Victorian novel. The main concern of the Victorian novelist was *society*; it was thought best to have access to everyone's thoughts and motives in order to create a clear and total picture of society. Victorian novelists would often reveal the thoughts of any and all characters in a given scene in the following manner:

> Henry arrived at two in the morning, feeling tired and numb (his interior state, his viewpoint). Kathryn greeted him at the door, thinking he looked like a drowned rat (her viewpoint). She showed him immediately into the library, where the old grandfather waited, pacing back and forth under the chandelier. He had been pacing there since noon, his stomach churning, his feeble mind in a terrible turmoil (the grandfather's interior state, his viewpoint).

The result was interesting and succeeded in giving the reader a powerful portrait of society and its workings, but, because of the constantly shifting viewpoint, the reader was not exposed to any character's viewpoint long enough to establish reader identification. The reader therefore lacked intimacy with these characters. For this reason, very few novels are written today in omniscient viewpoint.

LIMITED OMNISCIENT VIEWPOINT

The modernized version of omniscient viewpoint is *limited omniscient viewpoint,* a very powerful technique indeed. Limited omniscient viewpoint works like this: the author claims the right to go into the heads only of certain characters and not others. These selected characters, usually the protagonist and two or three others, are called "viewpoint characters." While the narrator is in the head of a character, because of the magic of identification, the reader is living that character's life. Unlike omniscient viewpoint, in limited omniscience the reader is not asked to switch viewpoint too often yet has the chance to enjoy intimacy with more than a single character.

This is how the Victorian scene above might be written in limited omniscience:

> When Kathryn opened the door, she was aghast: there stood Henry, wet, drawn, and tired. He looked positively numb from the cold. She showed him immediately into the library where her old grandfather was pacing, his back bent, under the chandelier. He'd been there, she knew, since noon. She guessed his feeble mind was in a terrible turmoil (all from Kathryn's viewpoint).

A severe form of limited omniscience is single viewpoint. It has most of the disadvantages of a first-person narrative, except that the narrator can relate events that happen out of the viewpoint character's purview.

CHOOSING A VIEWPOINT

When you sit down to begin your novel, you slip a sheet of paper into your typewriter or turn on your word processor. You next take out your notes, your character biographies, and your step-sheet; you put your premise up in neon on the wall and you think you're ready to go.

But then you find you can't write a single paragraph because you don't know what viewpoint to use. Knowing what the various options are—first-person, omniscient, limited omniscient, objective—does not necessarily make the choice easy. When is a first-person narrator appropriate and when isn't it? If a first-person narrator is advisable, can the protagonist narrate it? Should you use an omniscient narrator? Some authors use a combination of viewpoints, both objective and subjective, a first-person narrator and a third-person narrator in the same book. Would that work in your story, you wonder.

Many beginning novelists think that if they shift viewpoints frequently they are being creative. They fancy their work is experimental, even avant-garde. They use viewpoint not to enhance the story but to draw attention to their technique—exhibiting their genius, they imagine. This kind of tomfoolery is pretentious, if not downright silly.

To select the proper viewpoint, ask yourself not "what viewpoint?" but rather, "who can tell this story best?" The viewpoint you choose reflects the narrative voice and it is the narrative voice and not the viewpoint per se that is crucial. The selection of the narrative voice is based upon a consideration of genre.

Let's first define what is meant by "narrative voice." A fictional character has a "voice," a characteristic way of speaking ("Aw shucks, Wilbur, you dint hafta gimme dis here watch"). The narrator's characteristic way of speaking is called the narrative voice. The author may use either his own natural voice or one he assumes. The narrative voice, if the author is not using his own natural voice, is the voice of a sort of "character" that the author has invented to tell his story.

In the eighteenth and early nineteenth centuries, novels were written in the author's natural voice. If, say, Sir Edmond Ethelred Smithers were to write a novel, he would write it in the first person and his own opinions would be overtly expressed. He would discuss his characters as if they were acquaintances:

> Reginald was a burly fellow, polite and, I think, well-intentioned. He had a humane outlook on life, and treated his wife very well indeed, not beating her very severely unless she committed some egregious offense, such as raising her voice to her husband. One night, while they were alone, Reginald thought it might be a fine thing to see what his wife looked like without her clothes on. They had been married twenty-two years and he had never seen this spectacle, although he did glimpse her bosom for the briefest possible moment quite by accident one night the first year they were married when her dressing partition fell down in an earthquake . . .

The voice in the above example has taken a mildly sardonic tone, friendly, gossipy. It has a certain charm to it. This type of narrator, however, has mostly gone the way of the pterodactyl.

Sometime around the turn of the twentieth century, a time of mounting skepticism in the arts, it was noted that the author could not possibly know what went on while the characters were alone. In answer to this criticism, the omniscient narrator became "invisible." Authors no longer talked about their characters in a chatty, gossipy way. If the narrator commented on what he thought of a character or the developments of the story, critics would

holler, "Author intrusion!" Narrators ever since have simply related what was going on and have kept their opinions to themselves. Most books today written in the third person follow this
code, although there is no law that authors must abide by it. In
fact, many contemporary Latin American writers and some
American iconoclasts, such as Kurt Vonnegut, have resurrected
the old way of doing things to good effect.

Most authors who like making sardonic comments and oblique
observations have switched to first-person narration, where it is
acceptable for the narrator, because he is a character in the story,
to say whatever he damn well pleases.

NARRATIVE VOICE
AND GENRE

As was mentioned above, the narrative voice you choose depends
on your story's genre. Genre, you'll recall, refers to the "type"
of story you are telling: literary, mystery, crime, western, confes-
sional, mainstream, romance, science fiction, fantasy, and so on.
For most genres, you are probably well-advised to use author-
invisible, third-person, limited omniscient viewpoint. That's the
standard; it's what readers expect and what editors want. You
should deviate from the norm only for powerful and persuasive
reasons.

You might make such a departure for a folksy tale of hillbillies
and their feuds. It might be best told by a neighbor who saw it
all. The local color in the narration would lend flavor and spice
to the story, as well as help make it sound more as if it actually
happened, which would increase verisimilitude. A western might
be told by an old sourdough or by the hero's sidekick; a nurse
romance, by the nurse who falls in love with the handsome young
surgeon; a science fiction story, by a Martian.

When the narrator is anonymous and neutral, the reader buys into the story only if the story is completely plausible. The following passage is written first with an author-invisible, third-person narrator, then with a first-person narrator:

> Mary was a good housewife: neat, organized, ready with dinner at six o'clock when Bob came home. Bob was a good provider, a stable man, a churchgoer; he liked to help around the house. Mary did needlework, volunteered at church socials, and liked to watch television. They belonged to the Lions Club. But something was not quite right in their marriage. Mary was bored. It wasn't that she didn't love Bob and the kids, it was just that she had so much free time on her hands. So when she met "Sweet Jesus" Mahoney and he offered her a job as a hooker three afternoons a week, she thought, gee, I could get that new coat I've been wanting . . .

As you can see, this story is difficult to believe in the third person. Here is the same passage with a first-person narrator:

> Hey, the craziest damn thing's gone down in our town. There's this housewife, see, name of Mary Pringle, not too bad-looking, not too good-looking, who's married to this guy Bob, a guy I used to go bowling with down at Speedo Lanes. Anyway, one day Mary is having lunch downtown at Bing's and there's this guy there, flashy young dude name a "Sweet Jesus" who's running some girls out of the Seaside Ranch Motel, and

he spots Mary. I don't know what he saw in her, she was just a plain-Jane housewife, but anyways, he sits down at her table and says to her, hey, how'd you like to make some fast bread? Mary's astonished. She almost falls off her chair. But the guy says, look, I'm serious. I think underneath all that plain-Jane stuff you got some treasures worth marketing . . .

You can see how the believability of the story is enhanced by the narrator's amazement. His tone says, in effect, "Look, I wouldn't believe this either, but it's true." One of the reasons we believe that Sherlock Holmes has such extraordinary powers is that Dr. Watson tells us so.

If you reflect a while on which viewpoint would be best for your story and you still don't know, try telling the story from two or three different viewpoints, then put these versions away for a day or two. When you take them out again and coldly reread them, the right viewpoint will probably jump right off the page at you.

THE MAGIC OF IDENTIFICATION, THE GREATEST TRICK OF ALL

We are all voyeurs. Fiction gives us insight into other people as no other medium can. When we read fiction we participate in the lives of others at a much deeper level than when we read, say, a newspaper account. In fiction, we are intimate with the characters. Fiction can be more real to the reader than reality itself because fiction is the *essence* of life. In a fictional story, the reader is brought into the inner experience of the characters. If the writer is skilled enough, the reader will identify with the characters to the degree that, for the time he is reading the book, the real world will fade and the reader will be completely absorbed into the story world of the characters.

The novelist is a sort of magician, weaving a spell over the reader. To weave the spell, the novelist uses the magic called *identification*.

How, then, can you as the author work this magic?

First, as soon as you open your story, give your reader an emotional touchstone—plunge a character into an emotion-provoking situation. Fiction writing involves human characters, and human characters have emotions. You can touch your reader best if you introduce a character with problems the reader can sympathize with at the very beginning.

- Humbert Humbert is in the throes of love at the beginning of *Lolita*. He loves Lolita until it hurts. The reader feels sorry for him.

- Leamas is worried about one of his agents coming out of East Germany. The reader is drawn into his world immediately and worries along with him.

- *The Godfather* begins with a minor character watching the trial of two men who assaulted his daughter. The reader can pity him easily.

- *The Old Man and the Sea* begins with an old fisherman who has not caught a fish in a long time and is suffering hardship. The reader pities him as well.

- Flaubert begins *Madame Bovary* with a portrait of "poor Charles," Monsieur Bovary, who is to be cuckolded. The story begins with his being shamed in school. The reader pities him too.

- In A *Christmas Carol,* the emotion Dickens raises is not pity, but contempt—for Scrooge. It works well; readers loathe him.

Once an emotion (pity, contempt, fear) has been aroused by the opening, the characters should be plunged immediately into a developing crisis. If you've touched your readers' emotions, they will be interested, but true identification can occur only when the characters face choices *so that the reader can participate in the decision-making process.* If the reader is saying, "Come on, Harry, run for it!" or "Don't marry that clod!" the reader is identifying with the character. Identification comes when the reader pulls for the character to make the right choices.

There's a widely held belief that identification can occur only if the character is *admirable.* Humbert Humbert is hardly admirable. He loves a nymphet and marries her mother so he can be close to her. He lies, cheats, and murders. Hardly admirable qualities. Why do readers identify with him? Because he suffers. Because he struggles. Because he's human and his emotions have touched theirs.

You can kill the spell of identification just as easily as you can create it—if you lose the readers' sympathy for the character. You can lose reader sympathy by having your character commit acts of cruelty to another character with whom the readers identify more strongly or for whom they have strong sympathy. You can lose reader sympathy by having the character make dumb choices—acting at less than maximum capacity. The idiot in the horror story who responds to creepy noises by going into the attic armed only with a candle is an example. You can lose reader sympathy when a character seems too ordinary, is stereotyped, or doesn't struggle hard enough. The reader wants to cheer a fighter, not witness a milquetoast wallowing in, say, self-pity.

THE FINE ART OF
FLASHBACKING

The flashback is the most misused and overworked device in fiction writing.

Readers are totally absorbed by what happens next. That is one way storytelling works its magic. The author gets the reader interested in a character and situation, plunges the characters into conflict, and soon the reader is caught up in the characters' lives. The reader can't wait to find out how the mess the author got the characters into is going to turn out.

Say Sam Smoot, your hero, is finally coming to terms with his heroin addiction. He has entered a rehabilitation program. His wife has called off the divorce—maybe. You, as author, decide it might be a good time to flash back to the time Sam was four years old and fell off the swing, because that trauma is what caused all his insecurities, and you think the reader would be fascinated. So you write a magnificent flashback. What happens? The reader comes to the flashback and either skips ahead so he can find out what happens next in the "now" of the story, or throws the book in the garbage. Four-year-old Sam is not the Sam we care about. It's that simple. Readers find most flashbacks intolerable. Yet a lot of neophyte writers flash back like mad. Why? No one but the Creator of the Universe knows for sure, but there is a likely answer: they find the conflicts in the "now" of the story produce anxiety in themselves.

Writers identify with their characters just as readers do, even more so. Putting characters into conflict creates tension in the writer because he so strongly identifies with them. He becomes anxious. For relief, some writers go into a flashback where the conflicts in the "now" of the story have not yet arisen, and the conflicts in the flashback have no consequences because in the "now" of the story they are in the past. The writer can relax. In other words, a flashback is a device foolish writers use to avoid conflict.

One reason writers think this is okay is because of Sigmund Freud. Freud taught the world that traumatic experiences in childhood account for the neurotic behavior of adults. Ever since Freud first expounded his theory, writers have been psycho-analyzing their characters. At first, readers were fascinated by the insights about characters to be found in their pasts. But psychoanalysis is no longer a new phenomenon. Readers are no longer awed by a flash of Freudian insight. It's pretty old stuff. In other words, who cares that Melvin wanted to do it with his mother? We want to know what's going to happen when he tries to stick up the 7-Eleven at the end of chapter 4, so let's get on with it.

In *Professional Fiction Writing*, Jean Z. Owen claims that "some editors state outright that they will buy only those stories told in chronological order, with no regression into the past," while others, she says, "do not list the flashback as an actual taboo . . . most of them agree this literary device should be used only when absolutely necessary."

So, you ask, when do you know a flashback is absolutely necessary?

It's necessary if your character is about to be plunged into a situation in which he will act contrary to the way he has been acting up to that point in the story. Say a character is always coming on strong with women, but he does so only because he is really a shy person and is hiding the fact that he is unable to perform in bed with women. Now the character is in love with a woman. There's trouble ahead for him, but the only way for this to be made believable is to show the reader the bad experience which caused the character's problem. In other words, *the an-tecedent action must be relevant to the present story.* If the narrator simply told the reader about it, the reader might be skeptical and suspect the author of melodramatically contriving the hero's re-luctance. A flashback, then, is the only convincing way to reveal this facet of the character.

It may also be necessary when in the *now of the story* the character is unsympathetic, loathsome, or revolting, and the writer wishes to make him less so; perhaps even to make him admirable.

Dickens, for example, made good use of the flashback device in A *Christmas Carol* when the Ghost of Christmas Past forced Scrooge to examine his life. By using conflict with the Ghost in the *now* of the story Dickens was able to keep his reader gripped in a rising conflict and simultaneously examine the flashback scenes which shaped Scrooge's character.

Without these flashbacks the reader would never understand how Scrooge had become such a miser, and the reader's growing sympathy for Scrooge would not be as great as it is by the end of the story. Could Dickens have brought this out without using flashbacks? Perhaps he could have had Scrooge plead with the Ghost for mercy in the *now* of the novel. Scrooge might have claimed to be an abused child whose mother died giving birth to him, and whose cold-hearted father never forgave him. But such pleading might sound hollow given the callousness with which Scrooge treats the rest of humanity. Clearly, Dickens needed to show Scrooge as a young boy to allow the reader to empathize with Scrooge's loneliness, and the only way to do that effectively was on-scene, in a flashback.

Before you go ahead with a flashback, ask yourself if you can make the same impact on your reader through conflict in the *now* of the novel. If the answer is no, then the flashback is necessary, but remember that within the flashback all the same principles of good dramatic storytelling which apply in the *now* of your story—fully rounded characters, a rising conflict, inner conflicts, and so on—continue to apply.

FORESHADOWING

Foreshadowing is so important that Lajos Egri in *The Art of Dramatic Writing* makes it a type of conflict, along with "static," "jumping," and "slowly rising." Foreshadowing is not actually conflict, but rather the promise of conflict.

Here's an example of foreshadowing:

> Joe got out of bed, ate breakfast, loaded his gun, and set out for town.

This is foreshadowing because the reader thinks, "What's the loaded gun for?" A story question has been raised. Foreshadowing is the art of raising story questions. If the story questions are slight, the reader is mildly interested. If the story questions are great, the reader is gripped. You can slip in foreshadowing artfully, as naturally as breathing. Here is an example:

> Susie saw Eddie the first day of class and that night wrote in her diary, "If he doesn't take me to the prom, I'll throw myself off the water tower."

Here's another example:

> Joe stopped at the kennel the night after the fight with his neighbor, Emil, over the lawnmower. He asked the kennel owner how much for a pit bull terrier. The kennel man said four hundred dollars. Joe said it might take him some time to raise that kind of money, but he could, if he put his mind to it. That night, full of Kentucky fried chicken and Tennessee sippin' whiskey, sitting on the back porch and listening to

an owl hoot in the tree, he came to a decision . . .

You can also foreshadow in the narrative, apart from the actions
of the characters:

When Pete got off from work that night, he
had no idea any surprise awaited him in his car.
In fact, he didn't hear the snake hiss as he started
the engine.

Foreshadowing may also be used to get the reader through a
particularly dull stretch of narrative. With the writer of genius
perhaps there will never be a dull stretch in his story, but with
most journeyman writers dull stretches seem inescapable. Say
you're writing a novel. In it preparations are being made for a
trip, say, and certain significant actions which occur during these
preparations will play a large part later; the preparatory actions
must be shown even though these actions are not in themselves
dramatic. Say cheap rope is purchased and the cheap rope gets
the heroes stuck on a ledge on Mount Awesome. The decision
to buy the cheap rope is clearly an important one, but it only
becomes important later in the story. To interest the reader in
the buying of the rope scene, the later disaster may be foreshadowed. You could begin the scene like this:

When Rudolf went into the store to buy his
supplies, he had no idea that he was about to
make one of the biggest blunders of his life.

Such a line makes the reader perk up. What could the blunder
be? A powerful question has been raised in the reader's mind,
and, for the author's purposes, that's good.
A dull stretch may not last for just a scene; it may go on for

a chapter or more. Say, as an example, one of your characters, Jeffrey, has a history of emotional problems and toward the end of the story is going to do some wild things, including trying to scalp his future father-in-law with a power mower. However, in the beginning Jeffrey is as sweet as sugar, and responds to trouble by withdrawing sullenly into a shell. You suspect that the sullen Jeffrey will put your readers to sleep. The way to wake them up is to let them in on your secret, that the sweet, seemingly deeply religious, if not out-and-out pious, Jeffrey is a potential homicidal maniac. Now then, how can you foreshadow the coming storm?

You could do it in the author's voice, in narrative, as was done in the previous illustration involving the purchase of the rope:

> Jeffrey was on his way to church when he spotted the house where the little gray dog once lived. The dog he had killed one night in a rage. But that was then, and this was now. Now he kept his rages inside him, locked securely away where, he told himself, they would never get out again.

Another way to foreshadow is to have a character give a warning:

> Julie didn't know the old woman standing on the porch when she came home from shopping. The old woman was wrinkled and hunched over, pale as death. Her eyes bulged in their sockets, the pupils opaque as the cold eyes of a dead fish.
> "Are you the one who is to marry Jeffrey?"
> Julie nodded. "Yes. On Saturday."
> "You should know that he has the madness in him. It is in the blood."

> The old woman then turned to walk away.
> "Wait!" Julie cried. "How do you know?"
> The old woman stopped, cackled, and looked
> back over her shoulder. "I am kin, and I have
> the madness in me. That is how I know."

Use your minor characters to foreshadow the actions of the major characters.

You can also foreshadow actions of a major character through his own actions. What a character does under a little stress is very telling about what he might do under a lot of stress. Say he drowns a kitten that annoys him. Or say he digs his fingernails into the palm of his hand so that it bleeds and is momentarily fascinated by the flow of blood. Maybe he screams at someone for crossing in front of his car. That kind of thing.

Foreshadowing, remember, is a promise. If the promise is made and not fulfilled you are cheating the reader.

SYMBOLS—THE GOOD, THE BAD, AND THE UGLY

A symbol is a thing that has meaning to someone in addition to the meaning of the thing in itself. If you're describing a cowboy riding along chewing beef jerky, the jerky has meaning in itself. It means food. But jerky is not a symbol because it does not have any additional meaning.

Now, say, ten years later, the same cowboy is a successful oil man. He comes across a piece of beef jerky in a swanky restaurant on the day he is about to swindle his best friend out of his last million. He fondly reminisces about the beef jerky. He would no longer eat the stuff, but the beef jerky is a symbol to him of the past uncomplicated life when he was an honest working man. The beef jerky has been raised to the level of a symbol. It stands for something more than food. It is now a physical representation of simplicity, honesty, hard work. Let's call it a "life" symbol, because it has meaning in the "life" of the character. Here are some other examples of life symbols:

- In *Moby-Dick*, Melville raises the White Whale to the level of a life symbol. It becomes much more than just a whale; it is the living embodiment of evil.
- The "A" worn by the adulterous heroine of Hawthorne's *The Scarlet Letter* is a life symbol.
- The catching of the fish in *The Old Man and the Sea* is a symbol of manhood to the old fisherman. That is a life symbol.
- The lump of coal which he denies Bob Cratchit is a symbol of Scrooge's miserliness; when he is transformed at the end of the story, the full coal scupper Scrooge gives to the clerk is a symbol of his generosity. The lump of coal is a life symbol.

These life symbols are symbols not only to the reader, but to the characters as well. They are naturally occurring, in a sense. From the author's point of view they are "found" symbols. The writer, in the course of telling the story, finds symbols to help the reader focus on the conflicts and the issues. You'll find such symbols in all literature from every country of the world since the beginning of time.

Symbols have unfortunately been greatly abused of late, largely due to a school of literary criticism called "the imagists." The imagists are the progeny of the infamous "new critics" of the forties and fifties, those villains who preached that the reader, not the writer, was the author of the work.

To the imagists, a symbol can be more than a life symbol; it can be a "literary symbol." A literary symbol, unlike a life symbol, is not a thing that comes to have meaning to the character in the natural course of the story. A literary symbol has meaning only to the reader, not to the characters. Say that in a story whenever villainous characters are described, the author points out their shiny shoes. The shoes are symbols of evil. But to whom are they symbolic? Not to the characters, certainly. The author is making a game of his symbols. He's saying to the reader, let's see if you can find the hidden meaning in these shoes. Good writing uses devices that elucidate character.

Here's another trick of the imagists. An imagist will write a story that goes something like this: there's a red flag over the door where Henry and Henrietta are staying. There's a red rug in their room. She cuts herself accidently and bleeds red blood. Later, they fight; he spits red blood. Henry leaves in a red taxi wearing a red necktie. None of the characters in the story connects red to the events of the story. The writer is using red to "tie the story together" by its images. The image does not have to be a color, of course. It could be a potted plant, a 747, a moon of Jupiter, a pair of scissors, a cat, a pair of dirty socks. Anything. Such images are sometimes called "controlling metaphors." Using a device such as a controlling metaphor does not produce art, only artifice.

If you ever hear a writer say, "I've finished my story and now I'm putting in the symbols," you have found a writer who is under the perverse influence of the imagist school.

Imagist writers are also prone to use special symbols called "classical allusions"—veiled references to gods from Greek mythology or to the Bible. An imagist writer might name a character Bob Pantheon. His name is supposed to be a clue that he is god-like, because the pantheon was the whole gamut of the Greek gods. If you wish to write a damn good novel don't waste your time trying to find classical allusions. Character, conflict, and a slow rise to a climax are what count.

The appropriate use of symbol is this: if a character has a quest or a goal, it should be symbolized. If a character wants to escape loneliness, say, there should be a symbol of the escape—something the character sees and wants but can't get. Admittance to a certain club, perhaps, or a ticket for the Love Boat. If a character wants status, perhaps the symbol might be a pair of alligator shoes or a pink Cadillac Eldorado. Abstract wishes and desires are okay in real life, but they don't play well in fiction. An apt life symbol will focus the reader on the conflicts. That is the legitimate use and value of symbols.

7.

THE FINE ART OF GREAT DIALOGUE AND SENSUOUS, DRAMATIC PROSE

DIALOGUE: DIRECT AND INDIRECT, INSPIRED AND UNINSPIRED

"Hi,"Joe said to Mary.

Mary looked up from the book she was reading. "Hi," she said.

Joe shuffled his feet nervously. He was sure everyone in the school cafeteria was looking at him. "What ya doin'?" he asked.

"Reading."

"Oh. Reading what?"

"*Moby-Dick.*"

"Is it any good?"

"Just a fishing story."

Joe sat down. He ran his finger around his collar to wipe away the sweat trickling down his neck.

"Ah, I've got to ask you something," he said.

"I'm listening."

"Er, have you got a date for the prom?"

"I wasn't going to go to the prom."

"Gee, everyone goes to the prom. How'd you like to go with me?"

"Hmmm. I'll think about it, okay?"

"Don't think about it, do it! I'll get my old man's car. I'll have plenty of money."

"It sounds sort of all right."

"We can have dinner at Benny's Pizza Palace."

"Well, okay then."

The above scene is in the dramatic form. It has a central conflict because there is an opposition of wills (he wants to take her to the prom; she's reluctant to go), it rises to a climax, and the characters are orchestrated. Still, it stinks. Why?

First, the dialogue is completely uninspired. It is *direct* dialogue. Direct dialogue expresses exactly what is on the character's mind with no attempt on the part of the character to demur, use subterfuge, lie, be witty, and so on. Fine dialogue expresses the will of the character *indirectly*. Let's see how the same scene would read if it were written in indirect dialogue.

"I have to sit down here, it's my job," Joe said.

"Oh?" said Mary, looking up from the book she was reading.

"Yeah, the school pays me a buck fifty an hour to study in the cafeteria and serve as a good example."

"Sit anywhere you like, it's a free country."

Joe smiled at her and said, "I know your future."

"How would you know my future?"

"I read Tarot cards."

"I don't believe in Tarot cards, my family is Unitarian."

Joe took the cards out of his pocket and shuffled them. He put the first one down. He said, "You're going to be picked up at eight P.M. in a green Chevy Nova."

"I am?"

"The devastatingly handsome young man who's driving will be wearing a white dinner jacket with a plaid cumberbund."

"He will?"

"He will take you to the prom at this very school's gymnasium."

"Gee, the cards say all that, do they?"

"That and more." He put away the cards. "I don't want to ruin all the surprises."

"Am I being asked for a date?"

"Will you go with me?"

"The cards tell all, right? Then you ought to know."

Because Joe is using indirect dialogue, he comes across as more unique and interesting. A character at his *maximum capacity* will use clever, fresh, indirect dialogue. If you ever watch televison sitcoms you will hear mostly direct dialogue. It's one of the reasons they leave you feeling bored.

If you work on dialogue, your characters will display more wit, charm, erudition, loquaciousness, cleverness, and panache than you, the author. How is that possible? Because of the time factor.

What your characters say and do in a story seems spontaneous. They seem like real people saying and doing clever things. Joe just whipped out those Tarot cards and went into his patter. But the author of this book may have stayed up for two nights asking himself what Joe could do to impress Mary.

Have you ever been to a party where some clown is expounding, say, on the natural inferiority of women and you strongly disagree, but all you can think of to say is "You're full of it?" On the way home, you say to yourself that you should have quoted Simone de Beauvoir on the phenomenological vicissitudes of the existential cultural determinate theory of sexual differences in class and culture. That would have shut up that blowhard.

If your character had been in that situation, you could have thought it over for a while and come up with just the right thing to say. It might take you a week, but it would seem to the reader as if the character just came out with it spontaneously.

DRAMATIC MODES

Dramatic novels are written in three modes: dramatic narrative, scenes, and half-scenes.

In dramatic narrative, the narrator relates actions, shows character growth, and exploits inner conflict, but does so in a summary fashion. *Madame Bovary* is written almost entirely in dramatic narrative:

> Charles did not know what to answer; he respected his mother and idolized his wife; he considered his mother's judgment infallible, and yet everything about Emma was irreproachable to him. After the elder Madame Bovary had gone, he would timidly try to repeat, using her own

words, one or two of the mildest criticisms he had heard her express; Emma would quickly prove to him that he was wrong and send him back to his patients.

Meanwhile, following theories in which she believed, she made determined efforts to experience love. In the garden, by moonlight, she would recite to him all the passionate verses she knew by heart and sing him mournful adagios accompanied by sighs; but afterward she found herself as calm as before, and Charles did not seem to be any more amorous or stirred up.

Unable to produce the slightest spark of love in her heart by such means, and as incapable of understanding what she did not feel as she was of believing in anything that did not manifest itself in conventional forms, she easily convinced herself that there was no longer anything extraordinary about Charles's love for her. His raptures had settled into a regular schedule; he embraced her only at certain hours. It was one habit among many, like a dessert known in advance, after a monotonous dinner . . .

In a scene, of course, the narrator describes actions as they happened. Here's an example, again from *Madame Bovary*:

At dinner that night her husband found that she was looking well, but when he asked about her ride she did not seem to hear him; she sat leaning her elbow on the table beside her plate, between two lighted candles.

"Emma!" he said.

"What?"

"Well, I went to see Monsieur Alexandre this afternoon; he has a mare several years old, but still in fine shape, except that she's a little knee-sprung. I'm sure he'd sell her for three hundred francs or so . . . I thought you'd like to have her so I reserved her . . . I bought her . . . did I do right? Tell me."

She nodded. Then, a quarter of an hour later, she asked, "Are you going out tonight?"

"Yes. Why?"

"Oh, nothing . . . nothing, dear."

As soon as she was rid of Charles she went upstairs and shut herself in her room.

At first she felt dazed; she saw the trees, the paths, the ditches and Rudolphe; and again she felt his arms tighten around her while the leaves quivered and the reeds rustled.

But when she saw herself in the mirror she was amazed by the way her face looked. Never before had her eyes been so big, so dark, so deep. She was transfigured by something subtle spread over her whole body.

She repeated to herself, "I have a lover! I have a lover!" and the thought of it gave her a delicious thrill . . .

A half-scene is a dramatic narrative interrupted, blended with parts of scene:

Toward the end of September, Charles spent three days at Les Bertaux. The last day went past like the others, with the big moment being put off from one to the next. [Dramatic narrative to this point; now scene begins.] Monsieur Rouault was accompanying him a short distance before seeing him off; they were walking along a sunken road; they were about to part. The time had come. Charles told himself he must make his declaration before they came to the corner of the hedge; finally, when they had passed it, he murmered, "Monsieur Rouault, there's something I'd like to say to you."

"Go on, tell me what's on your mind—as if I didn't know already!" said Monsieur Rouault, laughing gently.

"Monsieur Rouault—Monsieur Rouault—" stammered Charles.

"As far as I'm concerned, I'd like nothing better," continued the farmer. "I'm sure my daughter agrees with me, but I'll have to ask her just the same. I'll leave you here and go back to the house. Listen to me now: if she says yes, you'd better not come in, because of all the people around; and besides, it would upset her too much. But I don't want to keep you in suspense, so I'll open one of the shutters all the way against the wall; you'll be able to see it if you look back over the hedge."

And he walked away.

Charles tied his horse to a tree, ran back to the path and waited. Half an hour went by, then he counted nineteen minutes by his watch. Suddenly he heard a sound from the house: the shutter had slammed against the wall; the catch was still quivering. [End of scene; return to dramatic narrative.]

He returned to the farm at nine the next morning. Emma blushed when he came in, but she forced herself to laugh a little in order not to seem flustered. Monsieur Rouault embraced his future son-in-law. They postponed all discussion of financial arrangements: there was still plenty of time, since the wedding could not decently take place until the end of Charles's mourning, the spring of the following year.

The winter was spent in waiting . . .

THE SHAPE OF THE DRAMATIC SCENE

Dramatic writing requires rising conflict. This is true not only for the dramatic story as a whole, but for the dramatic scene as well, whether it is handled in summary fashion in a dramatic narrative, or exploited more fully in a half-scene or a full scene.

A scene, because it has a rising conflict, must come to some sort of climax and resolution, even if the conflict is carried over into ensuing scenes. The core conflict within a scene does not have to be the same as the core conflict within the novel. The core conflict in a novel may be between a man and his wife; the opening scene may involve, say, a conflict between the man and his boss leading to his getting fired, an event that will in turn affect the core conflict.

A scene has the same shape as a story. It begins at a low point of tension and rises to a point of climax, followed by a resolution. Here's an example from A *Christmas Carol*:

> This lunatic, in letting Scrooge's nephew out, had let two other people in. [This is a bridge

from the previous scene. The new scene now begins.] They were portly gentlemen, pleasant to behold, and now stood with their hats off, in Scrooge's office. They had books and papers in their hands, and bowed to him.

"Scrooge and Marley's, I believe," said one of the gentlemen, referring to his list. "Have I the pleasure of addressing Mr. Scrooge, or Mr. Marley?"

"Mr. Marley has been dead these seven years," Scrooge replied. "He died seven years ago, this very night." [So far this scene has very little conflict. Scrooge has yet to find out the gentlemen are there to ask for money.]

"We have no doubt his liberality is well represented by his surviving partner," said the gentleman, presenting his credentials.

It certainly was; for they had been two kindred spirits. At the ominous word "liberality," Scrooge frowned, and shook his head, and handed the credentials back. [The tension is rising.]

"At this festive season of the year, Mr. Scrooge," said the gentleman, taking up a pen, "it is more than usually desirable that we should make some slight provision for the poor and destitute, who may suffer greatly at the present time. Many thousands are in want of common necessaries; hundreds of thousands are in want of common comforts, sir."

"Are there no prisons?" asked Scrooge. [Now he's getting nasty; they want his money.]

"Plenty of prisons," said the gentleman, laying down the pen again.

"And the Union workhouses?" demanded Scrooge. "Are they still in operation?"

"They are. Still," returned the gentleman, "I wish I could say they were not."

"The Treadmill and the Poor Law are in full vigor, then?" said Scrooge.

"Both very busy, sir."

"Oh! I was afraid, from what you said at first, that something had occurred to stop them in their useful course," said Scrooge. "I'm very glad to hear it."

"Under the impression that they scarcely furnish Christian cheer of mind or body to the multitude," returned the gentleman, "a few of us are endeavoring to raise a fund to buy the poor some meat and drink, and means of warmth. We choose this time, because it is a time, of all others, when Want is keenly felt, and Abundance rejoices. What shall I put you down for?"

"Nothing!" Scrooge replied.

"You wish to be anonymous?"

"I wish to be left alone," said Scrooge. "Since you ask me what I wish, gentlemen, that is my answer. I don't make merry myself at Christmas, and I can't afford to make idle people merry. I help to support the establishments I have mentioned—they cost enough; and those who are badly off must go there."

"Many can't go there; and many would rather die."

"If they would rather die," said Scrooge, "they had better do it, and decrease the surplus population. Besides—excuse me—I don't know that."

"But you might know it," observed the gentleman.

"It's not my business," Scrooge returned. "It's
enough for a man to understand his own business, and not to interfere with other people's.
Mine occupies me constantly. Good afternoon,
gentlemen!"

Seeing clearly that it would be useless to pursue their point, the gentlemen withdrew. [Point
of climax, followed by the resolution, including
Scrooge's emotional growth.] Scrooge resumed
his labors with an improved opinion of himself,
and a more facetious temper than was usual with
him.

Meanwhile the fog and darkness thick-
ened. . . . [Bridge to the next scene.]

The above is an example of a full scene. It begins when the
gentlemen arrive; the conflict rises to a point of climax; and it
ends with a resolution and a bridge to the next scene. Many
times it is not advisable to use a full scene, because at the
beginning of the scene the conflicts are not strong enough to
engage the reader. Say your character is about to ask the boss
for a raise. He makes up his mind to go in and see the boss
first thing the next morning. The end of the scene where he
makes up his mind can be bridged directly to the middle of the
following scene:

"You've got to get that raise, Joe, we need the
money for the baby! If you won't go in there and
ask, I'm leaving you!"

"Okay, okay, I'll ask, I'll ask, first thing tomorrow!"

He didn't sleep well that night and the follow-

ing morning [bridge to next scene], standing in
front of the boss [plunging right into the scene],
Joe felt his knees shaking while he stammered
his demand: "I get a raise, or I quit!"

The boss looked up at him and a wolfish grin
appeared on his face. "We're going to miss you
around here, Cogsgrove." [Climax of the scene.]

That very afternoon Joe bought the rope he
intended to use to hang himself. . . . [Resolution
and bridge to the next scene.]

Plunging into the middle of scenes speeds your novel along
and keeps the reader involved in the rising conflict. For varying
effect, a scene's climax might even be skipped. There are also
times when a whole scene might be omitted, either because it
would not have intense enough conflict, or for comic effect:

Joe made up his mind that morning there was
only one thing to do. All he had to do was borrow
his dad's old shotgun and go down to the local
liquor store, and that night he would have enough
to get to Hollywood, where he was sure to be
able to break into television. He waited until dark
before making his move, wearing his ski mask,
gloves, and running shoes. He parked his car
around the corner and walked into Fred's Liquors
at 9:00 exactly. At 9:28 exactly he was booked
into the city jail [skipping the actual holdup for
comic purposes].

When critics say a work is fast-paced, it is often because the
writer keeps his characters engaged in intense conflicts and cuts
directly into scenes with rising conflict. When you write your

novel, consider each scene and ask yourself whether part of the scene might be trimmed to speed up the pace.

DEVELOPING A DRAMATIC SCENE FROM THE FAMILIAR AND FLAT TO THE FRESH AND WONDERFUL

The following is a familiar situation, that of the police arriving on the scene of a murder and talking to the deputy coroner:

> Lt. Fisk pulled up in front of the house on Vermont Street and got out of his car. He walked up the steps and rang the bell. The maid opened the door after a moment and led the lieutenant to the solarium in the rear where the coroner's man was waiting. The coroner's man introduced himself as Herman Trippet and the two men shook hands.
> "Where's the body?" Lt. Fisk asked.
> "Right over here," Trippet said. Trippet was a tall man with a small mustache.
> The maid excused herself.
> Trippet showed the lieutenant the crawl space behind the couch where the body lay, covered with a white sheet.
> "Let's see it," Fisk said.
> "It's not pretty."
> Trippet pulled the sheet back, revealing the body of a woman in her early thirties. Her throat had been cut.
> "How long has she been dead?" Fisk asked.
> "Two, maybe three hours."

"Any sign of struggle?"

"No."

"Okay, when can you give me a full report?"

"It'll be on your desk by eight in the morning."

Fisk said: "Have you found the weapon?"

"No."

"Are the lab guys on the way?"

"Supposed to be here an hour ago."

"Leave the stiff till they come. I'll talk to the maid."

"Right, Lieutenant."

In this poorly realized scene there is no conflict, nothing fresh; the characters are stereotypes. It's a scene you might see on a television cop show. In addition, the writing has no color, no pizzazz. First, let's see what putting some conflict into the scene might do. We'll pick it up as the lieutenant enters the solarium:

"My name's Fisk," the lieutenant said, not bothering to put out his hand to the younger man.

"Trippet," Trippet said.

"You new?" Fisk asked.

"I been around a while."

"How come I ain't never seen you before?"

"Been working out in the valley."

"Still, I should have heard of you if you was any good."

"I'm good."

The lieutenant turned to the maid. "I'll send for you if I need you, Toots."

The maid nodded and backed out of the room.

"Where's the stiff, Trippet?"

"Behind the couch."

The lieutenant looked behind the couch.

"You find her like this with a sheet over her?"

"I brought the sheet."

"I don't like nothing changed; get rid of the sheet."

Trippet removed the sheet and the lieutenant looked at the wound in the corpse's neck.

"Give me the time, Trippet."

"I'd say it happened anywheres between two and three hours ago, Lieutenant."

The lieutenant lit a cigar. "I thought you said you was good."

"By tomorrow morning I'll be able to tell you what she had for breakfast and when she had her last bowel movement."

"Okay, Trippet, I'll look forward to that. I like to look forward to things. Where the hell are the lab guys?"

"They've been sent for, that's all I know."

"Get on the horn, tell them I give them five minutes to get over here or fannies will be kicked and heads will be cracked."

"Okay."

This is better because the characters have been put in conflict, but the dialogue is still too direct. Here's a rewrite, picking it up at the point, again, where the lieutenant meets the coroner's man.

"Fisk," Fisk said.

"Trippet," replied the other.

[A direct exchange.]

The lieutenant turned to the maid. "Ain't you got some furniture that needs dusting?"

[Indirect—translation: Get lost.]

The maid scurried out of the room. The lieutenant turned to Trippet.

"Where's Hennessy?"

[Indirect—translation: What are you doing here?]

"Hennessy got his gold watch last Friday." [He retired.]

"I guess they retired his experience with him." [You, Trippet, must be a greenhorn.]

"I been working the valley the last six months." [I got experience.]

"I never heard of you."

[How could you be any good?]

Trippet reddened. "I never heard of you, either."

Fisk laughed. Then he said, "Where's the package?"

[Translation: body.]

"Behind door number three," Trippet said, sliding the couch out. "And under curtain number one," he added, removing the sheet.

[Translation is obvious.]

Lt. Fisk bent over the body. "Looks like a job done by Mr. or Ms. Fastidious. I prefer them like this. I can't stand a hack job. You figure out any of the big W's?"

[Indirect—meaning becomes clear in Trippet's answer.]

"Can't help with the who, the what, or the why, but I got a fix on the when."

"I can figure that myself. Two hours, thirty minutes ago—by the rigor mortis."

Trippet nodded in mute respect.

"Hennessy used to tell me things," the lieutenant said, "and I listened."

[I got experience.]

Moral of this story: good dialogue should be in conflict, indirect, clever, and colorful. Now, what do you do if yours isn't? Read on.

HOW TO MAKE A GOOD EXCHANGE OF DIALOGUE OUT OF A NOT-SO-GOOD ONE

Most fiction writers write rough drafts of their book, then work it over. Especially their dialogue. After you've written an exchange of dialogue, look it over and ask yourself the following questions about *each* line:

- Is it in conflict?
- Is it trite?
- Can it be said better indirectly?
- Is the line as clever and colorful as it can be?

The following exchange takes place between Lucy and her husband Joe on the night he comes home after being fired as a purchasing agent. He doesn't want to tell Lucy, because their baby is due in three months and they have no savings. The exchange begins as he comes through the door:

Seeing his long face, Lucy says, "What's wrong, dear?"

"What makes you think something's wrong?"
"You didn't kiss me when you came through
the door."
"Didn't feel like it."
"You going to tell me what's wrong?"
"How come you're so nosy tonight?"
"Maybe I have a right to be nosy, I'm your
wife."
"But you're not my boss!"
With that, Joe storms out of the room.

Let's ignore the obvious jumping conflict for brevity's sake.

Now then, to rework this dialogue what we have to do is look at each line and ask the four questions. Consider the first line:

"What's wrong, dear?"

Is it in conflict? Yes, the question is a kind of attack; the character wants something. She wants information. It pushes the other character, Joe, to make a response.

Second question: is it trite? Answer: yes. Okay, so you have to ask yourself how it could be said a fresh way and still be in conflict.

How about, "Why the long face?"

That's even more trite than "What's wrong, dear?"

How about, "You look absolutely crumpled, darling!"

Okay? In conflict? Not trite? Can it be said better indirectly? Calling someone "crumpled" is already indirect.

Now, is the line as clever and colorful as it can be?

The only way to tell that is to brainstorm it for a few minutes and see whether you can come up with a line that is more clever and colorful. How about: "Looks like someone let the air out of your tires, darling." Doesn't appeal to you? Okay, stay with the "crumpled" line.

Then go on to the next line, Joe's response: "What makes you think something's wrong?"

Is it in conflict? Well it's a defense, sort of, but weak, and not too clever or colorful. And it's trite. The line scores a zero.

So you brainstorm it. How about: "Everything's ducky." Too trite? Well, maybe a little, but after a few moments of brainstorming you can't come up with a better line, and, after all, it is colorful and indirect and in conflict. You decide to go with it.

After going through a similar process with each line, the exchange will be transformed into something like this:

"You look absolutely crumpled, darling "

"Can't understand why, everything's just ducky."

"Then how come no kiss tonight?"

"Don't want you to catch my cold."

"You got the grumpies, not a cold—and the grumpies aren't catchable."

"Look, Lucy, rule number one in marriage is don't harangue the husband until he's been home at least thirty seconds."

"And rule number two is share thy secrets!"

"And rule number three is you're my wife, not my boss, so shove off!"

If this exchange were part of a novel it would no doubt need to be worked again, perhaps many times. "Crumpled" doesn't sound right, and "ducky" is too British for these characters. But by working it over it will get better. Most dialogue must be worked this way and, through challenging yourself to infuse it with more conflict and to make it fresher, indirect, clever, and colorful, it will get better and better.

THE COMMANDMENTS OF DYNAMIC PROSE

There are three commandments of dynamic prose. They are:

A. Be specific.
B. Appeal to all the senses.
C. Be a poet.

The following is a nonspecific description, the kind we all write on the first draft:

> When Mrs. Applegate arrived at the terminal, the train had already left. She paced back and forth on the platform, trying to figure out what to do. There were other stations down the line; perhaps she could make it to one of them in time to catch up with the train. She asked a cab driver. He shook his head. "No way," he said. "It can't be done."
>
> She paced some more. There had to be a way. She went back into the terminal and asked the conductor when the next train would be. Two hours, he said. She couldn't wait that long, she said.
>
> She paced some more. Then suddenly she had an idea. What if she chartered a plane? Yes! She could make it if she chartered a plane.

The scene doesn't have a "specific" in it. Here's the same scene with specific details included. Watch how it becomes more alive:

> When Beatrice Applegate arrived at the Reno Amtrak Terminal, she found the 5:15 for San

Francisco disappearing on the western horizon. She paced back and forth on the gray planks of the old platform, trying to think of what to do. Then it occurred to her that Verdi was only ten miles away and the 5:15 always stopped there for mail. She found a pencil-thin cab driver leaning against his battered old Plymouth reading a racing form. "A hundred dollars if you can get me to Verdi in fifteen minutes," she said, waving a bill in front of him.

The old cabbie thought it over, spit out a brown gob of tobacco, and said, "Can't be done," and went back to his racing form. Beatrice growled and went back to the platform to resume her pacing. There had to be a way. She checked with the round-faced station agent. "Next train west is the 7:10," he said with a nod. She paced some more.

It might have been the blue jay circling overhead that gave her the idea. Weren't they flying charter planes out of the Sparks Airport? She could get there in twenty minutes, fly to Marysville, and meet the train before it got to Sacramento!

This may not be Pulitzer Prize–winning prose, but it's certainly better than the bland version that preceded it. The generalities have been made specific. But the prose is not sensuous because so far it is only visually descriptive. Good prose appeals not only to our visual imagination, but to every other sense as well—smell, taste, touch, and hearing. Sensuous prose also should include references to the secondary senses—pressure, heat, cold, and so on, as well as the psychic senses, such as premonitions, déjà vu, and the like. Here is a demonstration:

When Beatrice Applegate arrived at the gray-shingled Reno Amtrak Terminal, she found the 5:15 for San Francisco disappearing around the bend to the west, its shrill whistle dissolving into the distance. The smoke from its engine lingered in the air a moment before being blown away by a hot gust of desert wind that chafed her cheeks and burned her nostrils.

She paced back and forth on the heavy gray planks, her spiked heels clicking rhythmically. What could she do? A dusty map tacked on the wall gave her the answer. Verdi was only ten miles away and the 5:15 always stopped there for mail. A yellow and black cab, an old Plymouth with rusted fenders, stood in front. The cabbie, a tired, dark-skinned Mexican, leaned against the fender reading a racing form. He smelled of marijuana and had an air of danger about him. She would have to take a chance. She waved a hundred dollar bill in front of his face. His eyes brightened with innocent greed.

"Get me to Verdi in time to catch the train and this is yours." He jiggled silver keys in his hand as he thought, then shook his head. "No es posible," he said sadly.

The third commandment, "Be a poet," is easily said, you say, but not easily done. You're right. And that's not the only problem. This commandment also has a subcommandment: "Don't be too much of a poet." Being a poet, for a novelist, means using figures of speech to good effect. Figures of speech include personification, hyperbole, metaphors, and similes.

Personification is giving human qualities to inanimate objects. "I love my car, but my car hates me." *Hyperbole* is exaggeration:

"My ex-wife has the compassion of a Nazi stormtrooper and the disposition of a crocodile." A *metaphor* is an implied comparison of one thing in terms of another: "She'd stopped dieting in May; by November she was a whale." "George stuck his hand in the dynamo and turned it into hamburger." Many metaphors seem so apt that they're overused and have become clichés: "He sees the world through rose-colored glasses." A *simile* is a direct comparison using "like" or "as": "After the horse stepped on it, the man's foot looked like a pancake." "Mary's boyfriend is as bland as oatmeal."

A good figure of speech will not only strike the reader as clever, but often will have a certain resonance. Dickens, for example, described Scrooge as "solitary as an oyster." Not only is it apt because an oyster is closed up in a shell, but because it's a slimy little creature as well. Nabokov's Humbert Humbert describes his first meeting with Lolita thus: "A polka-dotted black kerchief tied around her chest hid her from my aging ape eyes . . ." His eyes are "ape" eyes, not only because they are ugly, but because they are the eyes of a child molester, a beast. When we first meet Charles Bovary, Flaubert describes him as having "his hair cut straight across the forehead, like a cantor in a village church." No doubt that was the way cantors in village churches customarily cut their hair, but the simile resonates because a village church cantor is likely to be narrow, provincial, and dull, just like Charles. The Chief, the narrator of *One Flew over the Cuckoo's Nest*, describes McMurphy's voice as being "loud and full of hell," which is more than apt, because it isn't just his voice that's full of hell, McMurphy himself is full of hell. Later, the Chief describes Big Nurse's lips as "in that triangle shape, like a doll's lips ready for a fake nipple." Not only is the simile apt because the shape of Big Nurse's lips are the same as a doll's, but Big Nurse is doll-like in the sense that she isn't human.

How can you find apt figures of speech for your own writing?

You really don't have to be a genius. What it takes is practice. Whenever you write narrative, try to find as many apt figures of speech as you can. When you're writing a rough draft put them down whenever they occur to you even if they sound a little foolish; you can always tinker with them later. Whenever you have a vague adjective describing something, try to find a comparison to make the description more vivid, and try to make it resonate. If a character is tall, how tall? Tall as what? Smart, how smart? Smart as what? A puppy is cute. How cute? Cute as what? If you keep trying, you will find good figures of speech come more easily to you.

But watch out. Failure to use good figures of speech may mean that your prose will be a little bland. Using bad figures of speech, however, will make your narrative foolish, laughable, absurd, or garbled. Unless you're writing comedy, they'll stick out like pink elephants in a flea circus. Here are a few guidelines:

Don't use the oldies but goodies:

> blind as a bat/eats like a horse/dead as a doornail/a cold fish/cool as a cucumber/tight as a Scotsman/right as rain/flies off the handle/crying over spilt milk/a sea of faces.

Don't use similes in a long string:

> She was tall, like a telephone pole; and she was thin, like a reed; and her skin was soft, like velvet; her eyes, blue as the Pacific.

Don't mix your metaphors:

> He liked to bury his head in the sand and keep his light hidden under a bushel.

Make sure you use allusions your reader will understand:

> He smelled like SO_2. (The reader might not know that this is the chemical symbol for sulfur dioxide, which smells like rotten eggs.)

Don't stretch your comparison:

> His hands were gnarled like the roots of a stump, blackened by years in the earth, rough as if half-eaten by termites, yet hard and solid as good roots should be . . .

Be careful when you make a comparison that it does not resonate wrongly:

> The evening was pleasant and warm, the sky speckled like the cheeks of a smallpox victim.

When describing something revolting, the comparison may also resonate wrongly:

> He looked into the sewer, holding his nose against the stench, the green bubbles bursting through like Christmas tree ornaments.

Don't make your comparisons too confusing to visualize:

> The lines in her face were like a road map laid over the floor plan of the Pentagon.

Resist the extravagant:

> Her eyes were like Indian sapphires, set among South African diamonds by the craftsmen of Tangier.

Don't combine the figurative and the literal:

> Doubleday was the father of baseball and two sons
> and a daughter.

PROSE VALUES BEYOND
THE SENSES

Dynamic prose has certain properties that can be infused into
limp and pallid prose to give it strength, vigor, and color. For
example, good prose has time woven into its tapestry:

> She looked out over the barren, gray prairie
> where Chief Running Bear had met his death,
> and where the Seventh Cavalry had slaughtered
> a thousand squaws in a single day, and she was
> overcome with a profound sadness. Then some-
> one said, "Soup's on," and she turned and walked
> back across the sand-colored flagstones of the pa-
> tio and through the sliding door into the dining
> room where dinner was being served. By the time
> she had buttered her sesame roll, the chief, the
> squaws, and the butchers of the Seventh Cavalry
> were forgotten.

Another powerful device is to filter your descriptions through
viewpoint characters. You describe the scene, in other words, as
a character sees it. Sometimes the character misinterprets what
he sees:

> Norman woke up in his sleeping bag, yawned,
> and looked over Yucca Flats. The soldiers he had
> hidden from the day before were gone and only

the tower and the buildings remained. Now maybe
I'll find out what they're up to, he thought . . .

Good prose is active, not static. A scene should be changing,
or the perception of the scene should be changing. This is static:

> The red barn stood behind the house. It hadn't
> been used in years. The paint was peeling, the
> door was off its hinges, the pig pens had fallen
> down.

That is a still life. The rewrite below shows how the description
can be made dynamic:

> The red barn stood behind the house, its shut-
> ters banging on rusted hinges against the sides of
> the barn. The paint, flaking off in the breeze,
> fell like rust-red snowflakes in the empty pig pens.
> The squeals of the thousands of pigs raised there
> echoed now . . .

The admonition not to be too much of a poet is ignored in
the following passage:

> Mildred was a small-boned woman with a ski-
> jump nose and small, almost mouse-like ears.
> She walked very erectly, and when she talked it
> brought to mind the snow sparrow of Tibet. Her
> voice tinkled rather than tittered, like the snow
> sparrow. But there the bird-like quality ended.
> She had feet like a water buffalo. Not the African,
> whose feet are long and pointed, but the Siamese
> water buffalo, whose foot is as wide as the cedar

T h

de
s

8

REW
THE FI

THE WHY AND THE WHAT
OF REWRITING

"REVISION," William C. Knott says in *The Craft of Fiction*, is like "wrestling with a demon," where there "is no escape, for almost anyone can write; only writers know how to rewrite. It is this ability alone that turns the amateur into a professional."

Anyone who teaches creative writing knows Mr. Knott is absolutely correct.

The book you are reading presents a method for creating a damn good novel. You begin with a germinal idea. It might be an idea for a character, a plot, a location, or just a creepy feeling on the back of your neck.

Next, you jot down a few notes on how the idea might be shaped into a story. Say the germinal idea is a character, a daffy blonde. That's all. Upon meeting the real life Daffy at a party, you are intrigued by her and want to work with her. You start asking what ifs. What if Daffy fell in love with a Trappist monk? What if Daffy won a million dollars in a sweepstakes? What if Daffy joined the army? Soon you have a notion of what the core conflict might be. You write a few character sketches, flesh them out into biographies, and search for a premise, settling on something like, "daffiness leads to bliss." Then comes the stepsheet. From the stepsheet, the novel is drafted. And now rewriting and polishing, the final agonies. If you do all this conscientiously you can write a dramatic novel, right? Then you can sell it to a publisher and make a lot of money, right?

Well, no. Not exactly.

Time now for the truth.

If you have never written a novel, think of how hard it could be and then multiply it by a hundred. For some it is harder to write a novel than to row a bathtub across the North Atlantic.

Naw, you say. Not if you're a genius. Not if you've got talent.

If you're a genius or have talent, it's even harder.

How come? you say.

It's because a writer has a damn hard time evaluating what he has written, and unless he knows the strengths and weaknesses of a manuscript it will not be possible to turn a draft into a finished piece of work. So why is it so hard?

It has something to do with how the human mind works. When you read someone else's work, you see the faults, errors, and dead spots; poor characterizations, flawed metaphors, and so on, with no trouble at all. Read someone else's first draft; its faults will fly off the page at you. If a character is not well-motivated, you can sense it immediately—in someone else's book. You can tell when you're bored out of your mind—when you read someone else's book. Clichés abound in everyone else's work, but they will remain forever hidden in your own. And if you have a lot of talent, even if you are a genuine genius, it is even harder. Why is this? Only the Master of the Universe who made us knows, but it's true.

It isn't just blindness to the problems that will plague you when you try to evaluate your own work. You will automatically care about your characters because they are yours. Your reader may not. You will see your characters whole and unique in your mind's eye. Your reader may not. You will suffer when they suffer, cry when they break off their love affairs, grieve when they die. Your reader may only yawn.

To successfully complete a novel, you must learn to look at your work *objectively*. You must learn to see what your critics see. Then you must be able to change what you've written to make it powerful. This may mean trimming or eliminating some of your favorite scenes, or changing the plot, the characters, the style, the tone, the voice, the tense. Anything that needs to be done must be first faced, then reconsidered, then reworked.

Ouch, you say.

Right.

When you finish the first draft of your novel and give it to your mother, she will *love* it. So will your Uncle Harry. Your friends will like it and kid you about the millions you're going to make. But some of them might look you in the eye and say, "To tell you the truth I thought it was a little—I don't know —sort of dull in spots." When you try to pin them down, they shrug. You get a little queasy in the stomach because you think they might be right. Okay, you say to yourself, it's a little dull in spots. But what spots? And what can I do about it? First, you need a clear and objective evaluation of what you have. You have to know whether the effects you are striving for are working.

One way to find out is to seek out a group of writers and ask them what they think.

WRITERS' GROUPS AND HOW TO USE THEM

You'll find writers' groups everywhere. Writers come together like geese. It's part of their natures. There are basically three kinds of writers' groups: *puff*, *literary*, and *destructive*.

A *puff* group is fun to belong to. Whenever anyone reads a work, the criticism goes like this: "I loved the image of the flower growing up through the swimming pool. I loved every one of your characters more than I love my mother. Oh yes, and the green tortoise on the tie was a wonderful controlling metaphor."

This type of group often serves brownies and has a potluck every so often. After your work is read and discussed you will leave feeling like you're ready for the Nobel Prize. It's wonderful. Unfortunately, this type of group has ruined more writers than the McCarthy Committee. Stay for the brownies, bring soda biscuits to the potluck, but do not let them read your work, even if they pay you. You can gain nothing from flattery. It will destroy your determination by making you think your highly flawed first draft is a finished masterpiece.

A *literary* group is easy to spot. Ask the leader if he likes Joyce's *Finnegan's Wake*. If he has even read it past the third paragraph, you know you're in a literary group. This type of group will read your work and compare it to the masters. They will say things like "Oh, you should read Smirnoff's *Confessions of a Mad Madam*." You'll learn more about existentialism and imagists and Freudian allusions than you ever dreamed there was to know. Literary groups serve brie and white wine (the kind that comes in bottles with corks, never the kind that comes with screw-on tops). The cheese and wine are often very good. The criticism is invariably very bad. Knowing that you write like Bertha McFauncy will not help you an iota. The kind of writers you encounter here will be writing "experimental" prose. *Why* they are experimenting and what exactly the experiment is, most of them won't know.

The *destructive* groups are the only kind that are truly worthwhile. On your first visit to a destructive group, you'll think you've fallen into a new kind of psychotherapy where the idea is to destroy the writer's ego. You'll hear things like "Hey, come on, punch it up, your characters are acting like a bunch of pantywaists. These guys are supposed to be Marines, not hairdressers!" This is destructive criticism at its best. In some workshops, attacks on the author are allowed. You'll hear things like "You write vapid crap like this 'cause you're just a housewife. Get out in the world!" Or, "This reads like it could have been written by a Republican," and so on. Most destructive criticism groups, however, limit the criticism to the work. They have plenty of fun turning your precious prose into cole slaw. This is good. It's hard to take, but you don't make steel in a hot tub; you make it in a blast furnace.

Okay, at first you'll get mad. Maybe you'll cry. Or get drunk. Bang your head against the wall. But then, if you're prudent, you'll sit down, sort out the criticism, and start asking yourself what the others see that you don't.

You will have to be careful, however. Critics often try to get a writer to write the book they wish they could write. Be sure in your rewrite you are rewriting your book, not someone else's. Ask yourself what can be done to rewrite it to answer your critics without changing your premise. If you're writing a love tragedy, don't let your critics talk you into a happy ending. Be sure there is a *consensus* in the group. Don't let one or two vociferous members make you think you need rewrite where you don't. Ask the others what they think. If most of your critics agree, you probably will have to rewrite.

Then wait a few days, ponder the criticism, and think what you might do in a rewrite. Discuss it with your critics. Then go at it. Be ruthless in changing what needs to be changed, but do not change a word unless it is your firm conviction that you can make the manuscript better.

GETTING ALONG WITHOUT A GOOD GROUP

What if you can't find a destructive group, and you have neither the energy nor inclination to form one of your own? You have to become your own critic and try to get your friends to help.

One way to get the truth out of your friends, however reluctant they may be to give it, is to tell them the manuscript was written by someone else. Tell them you've agreed to critique it for a close friend and you just don't know what to say. You need help. This relieves your friends of the moral burden to be kind. If they think it's someone else's, they can say what they think without feeling guilty.

Whether or not you've told your readers the manuscript is yours, try to pin them down about any negative report to exactly what it was they didn't like—the characters, the situations, the pace (too slow, too fast), the clarity, and so on. Put them on the witness stand and give them a grilling worthy of Perry Mason. Do not ever voice disagreement with a critic. Let your critics say their piece. Never defend your work; it's pointless and will only make the critic hesitant next time. Feel free to ignore the criticism when you sit down to do your rewrite if you don't agree with it. You're the boss; it's your novel.

You'll get more out of your critics if you give them a list

of elements and have them rank the elements of your story in order of what they think was most "professionally handled." The list might include such items as plot, characterizations, use of language, and so on. Ask your critics to do the best they can and not to leave anything out. If six or seven out of ten list the same things near the top, you know what you're doing right. Those areas ranked lowest are where you need to focus your attention.

Another good diagnostic tool is to have each scene of your novel graded on an interest curve. Have your readers give you a grade of one to ten on every scene. If they are mildly interested it's a five; completely bored, a one; and totally gripped, a ten. If all your readers identify the same chapters or sections as under six or so, you know where to punch it up.

You can also make up a "Gallup poll" for your readers when they've finished the book. Ask them to vote for their favorite character, their least favorite character, the greatest scene, the worst scene, and so on. You can also ask them to recount the story to you; the parts that are left out most often are the parts where you've put the readers to sleep.

The best analyst of your story, potentially, is you. Self-analysis is a learned skill; with practice you can become a master. Since it is part of becoming a craftsman, you might as well start practicing it immediately. Reread your manuscript. Pretend someone else wrote it. Pretend it's a sick patient, and you're a doctor who's diagnosing its ills. One helpful method is to read your novel into a tape recorder and then play it back. Hearing it instead of reading it will transform your perception of it and might expose its faults. You might also try telling the story of your novel to a friend from start to finish. What you leave out and what you fumble over will help pinpoint weaknesses.

It is easier to be objective if you put your manuscript aside for some time before you begin to analyze it. Three or four months

would not be too long. Some writers wait a year. In the meantime
you can work on another one.

The most important thing about rewriting is your attitude.
When you rewrite you will have to be absolutely ruthless with
cuts, trims, and changes. As you examine each scene, keep in
mind the most important principle of rewriting: *if you suspect
it's lousy, it is.*

SELF-ANALYZING YOUR
STORY, STEP BY STEP

- The first question to ask yourself is: have you
  proved your premise? If you wanted to show that
  "greed leads to happiness," have you done it, or
  is it something else that leads to happiness in
  your story? Luck, say. If it's luck and not greed,
  you must rewrite your manuscript so that greed
  and not luck is what leads to happiness. You
  already decided before you began that the premise was one you believed in and that was worth
  proving. If you haven't proved it, you must go
  back and look at the stepsheet, look at the incidents, and decide on the changes that must be
  made so that the story will prove the premise. If
  you decide that with this character, as things
  turned out, it wasn't greed, but self-sacrifice at
  the end which led to happiness, you might consider changing your premise even at this late stage.
  But if you do, you must rewrite so that the story
  proves the new premise.
- Ask yourself whether you've touched the reader's emotions and allowed the reader to identify

with the character. Are there any scenes in which a sympathetic character acts cruelly or stupidly or duplicitously so that sympathy is lost?

• Are the characters in opposition? Are they always at their maximum capacity? Do they pass the "would he really" test in all situations? Are they securely placed in a crucible so they cannot disengage from the conflict? Do they have ruling passions? Are they well-motivated, decisive, determined? Have you avoided stereotypes?

• Principal characters should grow from pole to pole. Do yours?

• Have you plunged your characters into rising conflicts? Are the conflicts ever static? Do they sometimes jump?

• Are the conflicts adequately resolved so there is a sense of completeness? Have you left the reader with the feeling that the whole story has been told?

• Are the scenes and incidents varied; are repetitions avoided?

• Does the story begin at the correct place? Do you begin the story too early, so that it takes too long to get the conflicts heated up? Do you start too late, so that the reader is plunged into the heat of a rising conflict without first having a chance to become intimate with the characters?

• Do the events of the story grow out of one another? Is the reader able to clearly follow the A-B-C-D of events?

• Is the climax revolutionary? Is it satisfying? Does the climax-resolution have a surprise in it? Has the climax-resolution been exploited for powerful emotions?

- Is there some poetic justice or irony? If not, could there be?
- Does the story show many facets of the important characters? Are various emotional states explored? Are the characters fully revealed at the end?
- Are there any anticlimatic events? If so, cut them.
- Ask yourself whether you've chosen the proper narrative voice. Does it grate? Is it preachy? Would it help to tell this story in another viewpoint?
- Are all flashbacks absolutely necessary?
- Have you run away from conflicts that ought to be exploited? Have all significant actions been fully described?
- Are the conflicts symbolized, where possible, with appropriate life symbols?
- Check each scene. Does it have a rising conflict? Is it as exciting as it could be? If it can be cut without ill effect, it should be cut.
- Check every line of dialogue. Is it in conflict? Does it further the characterizations? Does it further the story? Is it fresh? Is it colorful? Is it the cleverest thing the character can say?
- Is the writing sensual, appealing to taste, smell, hearing, sight, touch, and the sixth, or psychic, sense? Are opportunities for humor exploited? Is passive voice used when it should be active? Are "to be" verbs used when more active verbs would serve better? Is the writing specific and concrete rather than generalized? Is there time and textural density to the writing? Is the writing forceful and sure, or limp and pallid?

It has been said that Ernest Hemingway would rewrite scenes until they pleased him, often thirty or forty times. Hemingway, critics claimed, was a genius. Was it his genius that drove him to work hard, or was it hard work that resulted in works of genius?

9.

THE ZEN OF
NOVEL WRITING

ON BECOMING
A NOVELIST

IF YOU go to dental school you will take a state exam when you finish and, upon passing, you will be given a license to practice dentistry. In order to take the test, you must have first submitted to a rigorous course of study, done thousands of hours of supervised work in people's mouths, taken hundreds of exams, and paid a lot of money. When you're finished, you will be called "Doctor," and your cup will runneth over with drilling, filling, and billing. If you do good gold crowns, play soft music in the waiting room, have a receptionist with a sympathetic smile and a soothing voice, you may even become rich.

In the course of your studies you will have been transformed from an ordinary citizen into a Doctor of Dental Surgery. You will even begin to think of yourself as something more than an ordinary citizen. Someone will ask you who you are and you will say, "Sam Smoot, Doctor of Dental Surgery."

For novel writing, unlike dentistry, there is no course of study you can pursue and, when finished, say "I'm a novelist." You can get an M.F.A. in creative writing, or a Ph.D. in the modern novel, but that won't make you a bona fide novelist. To be a novelist, you have to get published.

Being an unpublished novelist has about as much social acceptability as being a shopping bag lady. Should the word get out about you, your friends will snicker. Your neighbors will whisper about you. Your Uncle Albert will try to talk you into becoming a chiropractor. Your Aunt Bethilda will take you aside and lecture you on the grim realities and responsibilities of adulthood. Your creditors will break out in hives. Your mother will be sympathetic, but late at night her eyes will flood with tears as she tries to figure out where she went wrong.

It's a sad fact of life, but to be an honest-to-goodness novelist you must have that honor conferred on you by a publisher. But remember this: each and every bird is first an egg, and each and every published novelist is first an unpublished novelist—even the great ones, Ernest Hemingway, Leo Tolstoy, Virginia Woolf, and James Joyce included.

There are several strategies for avoiding the stigma attached to proclaiming yourself a would-be novelist. One is to tell people you are a writer, but not to admit that what you're writing is fiction. Suppose you're writing a murder mystery in which the victim is a prostitute and the murderer is a college professor. You can tell everyone you're writing a book about sexual mores and morbidity in academia. That sounds like a good subject for a nonfiction book. Your friends will be impressed. It's okay to be a nonfiction writer because it's assumed that nonfiction writers are hard-nosed practical people who take life seriously. Besides, it is popularly believed—possibly with some justification—that anyone who can spell well can write a nonfiction book, so no one will doubt that your project has merit.

Another way to camouflage your novel-writing pursuits is to enroll in an English Literature degree program someplace and take only snap courses. As long as it looks as if you're working for a degree no one will ask what you're doing locked in your study all day and half the night. If they ask you why you're banging away so hard on your typewriter, tell them you're writing a thesis. Everyone knows that's a sensible thing to do.

Some novelists at the beginning of their careers go completely underground. These "closet" novelists tell *no* one. They hide their manuscripts behind the refrigerator. They write in longhand so no one will hear the clacking of typewriter keys. Nobody knows the closet novelist even reads novels, let alone writes them. Their spouses may think they are keeping a lover in the basement or the garage, or wherever it is they "do it."

Any of these methods will work. The alternative, the "John Wayne Solution," is a bit tougher. The John Wayne Solution is this: grit your teeth, rock back on your heels, stick your thumbs in your belt, and just say it—*I'm writing a novel, and if you so much as smirk I'll punch your lights out, pilgrim.*

You get the idea.

WHAT COUNTS MOST—
AND IT AIN'T TALENT

We are all something else besides novelists, but if you are not a novelist in your heart, at your core, you are a dilettante and should not bother trying to be a novelist. Being a novelist is not just a matter of reading a book of technique and fiddling around at your typewriter putting little blotches of ink on paper. If you were to list the qualities a person needs to become a novelist, what would you put first? A college education? Charles Dickens, Jane Austen, the Brontë sisters, and Daniel Defoe never attended college. Neither did many modern writers of note: Ernest Hemingway, Truman Capote, Dashiell Hammett, Ambrose Bierce, and Willa Cather, to name just a few.

What about talent? If you attend writers' conferences and writing workshops around the country, you will soon see that there is no shortage of talent in America. Most anyone who puts his or her mind to it can write a cogent sentence and find fresh metaphors. Many can invent interesting characters and dazzle you with snappy dialogue. Some can even tell a crackling good story without ever reading a book on how it's done. When you look at their work, raw and unpolished, your heart will beat fast and you'll think you've discovered a genuine talent.

But most of these folks with so much raw talent will not make it as novelists. Why? Because they lack what's truly necessary: self-discipline, dogged determination, and stick-to-itiveness. Talent just gets in the way, because if you have talent you expect writing a novel to be easy and it isn't, no matter how much talent you have.

The writing of a novel takes a great deal of time and the expenditure of a great deal of emotional and mental energy. Time normally spent with friends and loved ones will have to be sacrificed. Few novelists play golf, go bowling, or watch much television. Novel writing is like heroin addiction; it takes all you've got.

In *The Craft of Fiction*, William C. Knott asks the rhetorical question, "How much of a commitment is required?" His answer:

> You must make the kind of commitment that will effectively subordinate almost every effort and interest (in your life) to the mastering of the craft.

Here is what happens to the vast majority of people who want to write novels:

They start out having a vague dream. They read about the writer's life: Hemingway fishing in the Gulf, Faulkner drinking his way through Hollywood, the wild parties, the sex orgies, the drugs, consorting with the rich and famous on Broadway. Most of this stuff is dreamed up by publishers' publicity departments and embellished by academic biographers who hope to make their books more salable by romanticizing the subjects' lives. If you want to read some really creative literature, read the biographies that deal with the sex life of Emily Dickinson. No kidding, there are people around writing books like that.

The truth of the matter is, most writers lead rather dull lives. They spend most of their time squirreled away in a basement or an attic with a word processor writing and rewriting, paranoid that the public might find their finished product silly, trite, or stupid. Some writers occasionally go to parties, but at the parties they're thinking about their writing. Knowing everyone expects them to be witty and profound, they usually keep their mouths shut, unless they are tanked to their blowholes, because anything they say will be weighed, judged, and misquoted.

The message is this: writing itself is not glamorous, exciting, or romantic. It's hard work. Rewarding, yes. But damn hard.

It is also a lonely process. It's a struggle with your own creative powers and self-doubts. Sometimes the writing flows out of you, gushing like rapids down a mountain gorge. Other times your head feels like a block of concrete and you can't squeeze anything out of it. Sometimes you reread what you've written and you think you could train your dog to do better. Other times you know what you've done is brilliant beyond your wildest expectations; you show it to your agent and he suggests you maybe should try a nurse romance.

No wonder the suicide rate among writers is high.

THE MATHEMATICS OF
NOVEL WRITING, OR
TO GET THERE,
KEEP PLUGGING, EVEN IF
YOU'VE GOT A HANGOVER

Any writer who is any kind of writer at all writes on some kind of schedule. The numbers are with you. Say you have a job, eight miserable hours a day, five days a week. An hour and a half each way commuting, one hour off for lunch. You make goddamn widgets all day. When you get home you're tired. You've got to give a little time to the spouse, you've got to sleep eight hours a night, you've got to go shopping, you've got to go to the dry cleaner, the bank, the dentist twice a year, and that leaves what? It leaves forty hours a week for the *average* American to watch television. Say you're a hardship case and only watch twenty hours a week. Okay, if you cut out the TV watching— which isn't doing you a bit of good anyway—you can write a novel, complete, ready to go to the publisher, in one year. Between the ages of thirty and seventy you can write *thirty-nine* novels and be one of the most prolific writers who has ever lived. Name five authors in the history of the world who have written thirty-nine novels. Not that many, are there? Hemingway wrote, what? Ten? Tolstoy, four or five?

Thirty-nine novels? Naw, you say, can't be done. Listen: if you plug away at it conscientiously, you will write at least two pages of rough draft an hour. A caterpillar can write two pages an hour. Some writers write rough draft at ten to twelve pages an hour. But let's say you are slow and two pages an hour is the best you can do. Okay, it takes one month at forty pages a week to write 172 pages of biography and stepsheet (2 pages per hour × 20 hours per week × 4.3 weeks = 172). Now you begin your first draft. Say it's going to be a four hundred-page book. A first draft will take ten weeks (2 pages per hour × 20 hours per week

× 10 weeks = 400). You have completed the biographies, step-sheet, and first draft in 14.3 weeks. Now you have to do a second draft: ten more weeks. Then a third draft: ten more weeks. At 34.3 weeks into the year you are ready to start polishing. You want to make it perfect, so you polish for two months, or 8.6 weeks. The total time is 34.3 weeks for biographies, stepsheet, and three drafts, plus 8.6 weeks for polishing for a total of 42.9 weeks. You now have 9.1 weeks left over in the year to take a vacation to Hawaii.

Of course not all writers write rough drafts. There are perfectionists who ponder every syllable as they compose. A perfectionist may only be able to complete one page every two or three hours, but what a page! In a week, ten to twelve pages is their maximum. The perfectionist's work won't need much rewriting, maybe just a little polishing. This adds up to over five hundred pages a year. In a year and a half the perfectionist can turn out a masterpiece even if *half* of what he writes ends up in the waste basket. In fifteen years, ten masterpieces. Even a perfectionist can be as prolific as Dickens.

The next time someone tells you they'd like to write but don't have time, ask them how much television they watch.

The secret of finishing a novel is regularity. Do it at the same time each day. You must say *nyet* to everything and anything that interferes with that time. No phone calls, no neighbors stopping by, no nothing. You can't work in the middle of a floating cocktail party. If somebody calls, let your answering machine get it. If a good movie is on television, sorry, you'll have to see it some other time. If your goldfish dies, you won't have time to attend the funeral. Even a hangover is not an excuse. The assembly line must keep rolling.

Some writers do not work well on a schedule. They simply set production goals. They write, say, twelve hundred words a day, period. Either way, it doesn't matter as long as you work your plan and it gets the pages done.

WHAT TO DO WHEN YOUR
MUSE TAKES A HOLIDAY

Writer's block is real. It happens. Some days you sit down at the old typewriter, put your fingers on the keys, and nothing pops into your head. Blanko. Nada. El nothingissimo. What you do when this happens is what separates you from the one-of-these-days-I'm-gonna-write-a-book crowd.

When you find you can't get going, don't panic. The faint-hearted will panic and run to the nearest bar, hoping to lubricate the creative pathways. That will work, but the loss of motor control adversely affects the product. You'll have to throw out almost everything you write while inebriated. The same goes for weed and nose candy and speed. Sure, Edgar Allen Poe wrote when he was schnockered to the gills, but he died at forty, incoherent and wetting on himself. Besides, he was the exception. James A. Michener does it sober. He's still cranking out damn good novels and he's past eighty.

If you do get blocked, the most important thing to remember is that writer's block happens to everyone and it is nothing to worry about. What you have to do is get the adrenaline going. Start retyping what you've already done to get warmed up. Play hot music; that might help. Read aloud what you've already written; that sometimes helps. Whatever you do, don't put the writing off. Keep pounding on that keyboard even if all you're producing is gobbledygook. You *will* work through a writer's block if you keep at it! You will never work through it if you walk away from your typewriter. That will only make it easier to walk away next time.

Do not confuse writer's block with other emotional states that interfere with your writing such as anger, grief, illness, laziness, horniness, and so on. True writer's block has four primary causes: not knowing your characters well enough, trying to edit and write at the same time, fear of failure, and fear of success.

Once you begin drafting your novel, the characters will come to life and have a will of their own. A character you don't understand well enough may rebel when you try to have him do something it is not in his nature to do. Say you've planned in your stepsheet to have a character steal some money at one point in the story. You start to write the scene, but the character refuses to walk into the bank with a gun in his hand. If you have created characters different from the ones you thought you were creating, you will have a difficult time getting them to do what you want them to. Your characters simply will not move. You can't make them say anything. It feels like your mind is constipated. You panic. This is a class-one writer's block.

The first thing to do when you hit a class-one writer's block is to interview your characters and find out whether they refuse to move because you're trying to make them do things it just isn't in them to do. You may have to give them stronger motivation or you may have to change your stepsheet. Either way, as soon as you've dug a little into the character the solution will be obvious and you'll be back in business. Your writer's block will vanish.

Trying to write and edit at the same time creates class-two writer's block. When you write, you have to first draft your novel without worrying whether every i is dotted and every t is crossed. The manuscript isn't going to be perfect; it's only a draft.

Later, during the rewriting phase, you will be a perfectionist, questioning every syllable and continually asking yourself whether you suspect it's lousy. When you're drafting, you're obviously going to see things wrong as soon as the ink hits the paper. This drives some writers bonkers. They immediately start to make corrections. Result: nothing satisfies them. Progress stops. Soon they can't put anything down on paper without cogitating about it. Then they immediately begin to correct their corrections. They develop a fear that they will never write anything beautiful and flawless again; they end up not being able to write a word.

The cure for this is to write with your monitor off, if you have a word processor, or with the lights off if you write longhand or type. Simply refuse to look at anything you have written until the last page is done. Period. If you try this method, your class-two writer's block will disappear.

Fear of failure will create a class-three writer's block. This usually happens close to the end of the manuscript when the writer looks into the future and sees a rejection slip awaiting him. The writer so hates getting rejected or ignored, at least subconsciously, that the writing just stops somewhere around the middle of the last chapter.

A class-three writer's block can be unblocked by shouting. Shout at the top of your lungs that nothing is going to stop you no matter how many damn rejections you get. Act as if your typewriter or computer is at fault. Scream at it. Things will start moving again.

Fear of success is more difficult. Why the hell would anyone fear success, you want to know. Sounds stupid.

Strange things happen to you when you become successful. Your spouse will treat you funny. Your unsuccessful friends will envy you. Strangers will want to get you into arguments. Everyone will ask questions about where you get your ideas. About how much money you make. About what you're working on now. They'll ask you about their favorite authors, and when you say you haven't read them they'll act as if you're stupid because their favorite author is ten times better than you. And how come you didn't get on Johnny Carson? How come *Time* or *The New York Times* didn't review your book? You'll be the center of attention, so what's wrong with that?

Some psychologists claim that standing up in front of a group to speak is the number one fear in America. People dread it more than death. Why is that? People fear being noticed, being the center of attention in a room full of people. A successful author is noticed. A successful author is often the center of attention in a room full of people. The not-yet-successful author looks ahead to that with dread. This is what fuels a class-four writer's block.

If you're afraid of success, go back to page one and put someone else's name on the manuscript. Write under a pseudonym. Many writers do. You could be living next door to the number one writer on *The New York Times* bestseller list right now and not even know it. There is no reason to fear being a celebrity. You can be a writer and pass that all up.

A class-five writer's block is caused by a combination of two or more of the above. You'll have to keep trying solutions until you find the right combination. Maybe even get a shrink.

WHAT TO DO WHEN THE JOB IS DONE

You will know when your novel is finished. You will feel like throwing up whenever you look at it. You will be at the point where further rewrite just changes things around; it no longer makes the novel better. Only different.

Now the thing to do is have it copy-edited by a grammarian who can spell, and have it professionally typed. There is a standard way to prepare and mail a manuscript, which is described in several books you can find at your local library. The most popular is *Writer's Market*, put out every year by *Writer's Digest*. Be sure to follow the standard; this is no place to get creative.

Your job now is to find an agent. If you've written a salable manuscript, you *will* find an agent. You will find an agent even if you've written a *possibly* salable manuscript. The way to go about finding an agent is this:

First, use writer friends. If they have agents, ask them to recommend you. If you can't get a recommendation, get a list of all known agents from the library. Write to them, including a brief synopsis of the book, a sample chapter, and a cover letter telling them about yourself, your educational background, any previous publications (including nonfiction), and the training you've had in writing fiction—including workshops you've attended and classes you've taken. Send all that along with an SASE, a self-addressed, stamped envelope.

When an agent expresses an interest, call and say you'll not send the book to another agent if you can be assured of a quick answer. Play fair with agents; they'll usually play fair with you. Court only one at a time. Agree to give them the manuscript only if they promise you a quick reading. If an agent keeps the book for more than a month, insist that he read it quickly or send it back.

Once you have an agent, let the agent work on selling the manuscript, negotiating the contract, and keeping track of your royalties. You get busy on the next one.

Bibliography

ARISTOTLE. "The Poetics" in *The Basic Works of Aristotle*. Edited by Richard McKeon. New York: Random House, 1941.

BAKER, GEORGE. *Dramatic Technique*. New York: Houghton Mifflin, 1919.

DICKENS, CHARLES. *A Christmas Carol*. New York: Simon and Schuster, 1939.

EGRI, LAJOS. *The Art of Dramatic Writing*. New York: Simon and Schuster, 1946.

FLAUBERT, GUSTAVE. *Madame Bovary*. Translated by Lowell Bair. New York: Bantam Books, 1959.

FOSTER-HARRIS, WILLIAM. *The Basic Formulas of Fiction*. Norman: University of Oklahoma Press, 1944.

———. *The Basic Patterns of Plot*. Norman: University of Oklahoma Press, 1959.

FREYTAG, GUSTAV. *Technique of the Drama*. Chicago: Scott, Foresman and Company, 1894.

HEMINGWAY, ERNEST. *The Old Man and the Sea*. New York: Charles Scribner's Sons, 1952.

HULL, RAYMOND. *How to Write a Play*. Cincinnati: Writer's Digest Books, 1983.

KESEY, KEN. *One Flew over the Cuckoo's Nest*. New York: Viking Press, 1962.

KNOTT, WILLIAM C. *The Craft of Fiction*. Reston: Reston Publishing Co., 1977.

LE CARRE, JOHN. *The Spy Who Came in from the Cold*. New York: Dell Publishing Co., 1965.

MACGOWAN, KENNETH. *A Primer of Playwriting*. New York: Random House, 1951.

MALEVINSKY, MOSES L. *The Science of Playwriting*. New York: Brentano's Publishers, 1925.

NABOKOV, VLADIMIR. *Lolita*. New York: G.P. Putnam's Sons, 1955.

ORVIS, MARY BURCHARD. *The Art of Writing Fiction*. New York: Prentice-Hall, 1948.

OWEN, JEAN Z. *Professional Fiction Writing: a Practical Guide to Modern Techniques*. Boston: The Writer, Inc., 1974.

PECK, ROBERT NEWTON. *Fiction Is Folks*. Cincinnati: Writer's Digest Books, 1983.

PRICE, W. T. *The Analysis of Play Construction and Dramatic Principle*. New York: W. T. Price, Publisher, 1908.

PUZO, MARIO. *The Godfather*. New York: G. P. Putnam's Sons, 1969.